KIM IL SUNG'S CHILDREN

Untold Stories of a Documentary Film

KIM DEOG-YOUNG

poppypub

김일성의 아이들 KIM IL SUNG'S CHILDREN
by Kim Deog-Young
Copyright @ 2021 by 김덕영 Kim Deog-Young
Photographs by Lim Sooyoung
All rights reserved.

First published in Korea in 2021 by Docustory
English Translation Copyright @ 2023 by POPPYPUB LLC
This English translation edition is published by Poppypub LLC arrangement with Docustory
All rights reserved.

No part of this publication may be reproduced, stored or transmitted in any form or by any means, electronic, mechanical, photocopying, recording, scanning, or otherwise without written permission from the publisher. It is illegal to copy this book, post it to a website, or distribute it by any other means without permission. This book is published with the support of Publication Industry Promotion Agency of Korea (KPIPA).

Translated by Alex Lee

Published by POPPYPUB, Fort Lee
www.poppypub.com
poppypub is a trademark of POPPYPUB LLC.

Library of Congress Control Number: 2022951097

ISBN 978-1-952787-28-7 (hardcover)
ISBN 978-1-952787-24-9 (paperback)
ISBN 978-1-952787-25-6 (ebook)

Shortly after the Korean War in 1950,
North Korea emigrated war orphans
to several countries in Eastern Europe
under the name of 'consignment education'.
This story is a record of
their hidden history.

— Movie *Kim Il-sung's Children*

CONTENTS

PROLOGUE
When records disappear, history is also forgotten 1
Routes of the migration and repatriation of North Korean war orphans 7

CHAPTER 1 Children from North Korea
Traces of North Korean children accidentally discovered 10
Unlocking secret documents 16
Photo album of hidden history 19
Reasons why we need a miracle 23
North Korean children's dormitory, Valeč Castle 29
The first impressions 33

North Korean children's report cards 38
War trauma 44
Angel on the road: Marie Kopecká 50
When records disappear, history is forgotten 55
I want to go back to my European home 63

CHAPTER 2 Language doesn't matter when you meet good people
South and North Korea dealt with war orphans in different ways 70
Lebensborn: The Nazi ethnic cleansing plan 75
The 1950s: The Cold War and regime competition 78
Trans-Siberian special train 81

Hidden history   85

Small army   89

Defeat was death   92

Fierce offspring   95

Walk to Europe   100

Language doesn't matter when you meet good people   103

Friendship to love   107

CHAPTER 3   Candles for the living

Georgeta Mircioiu: a woman waiting for her North Korean husband   114

Korean dictionary with 160,000 words   117

Dramatic life journey   122

Cho Chung Ho: A North Korean man   127

Secret love   131

Living in Pyongyang as a foreigner   135

Time of chaos   138

Exclusion campaign   141

Deportation and forced separation   143

Last family photo   147

Death of Cho Chung Ho   150

Unresolved questions   153

European women waiting for their husbands   157

Candles for the living   160

To Gigi   163

Flower basket—it's pretty!   166

Father, be strong!   170

CHAPTER 4 1962: The year North Korea closed its doors
Kim Il Sung's visit to Eastern Europe in 1956 and his clash with factionalists 178
Distorted society 182
Master of purging and removal of political enemies 187
The Hungarian Revolution 190
The winds of change in Eastern Europe 192
Escaping the dormitory 196
Closed group society 199
Group defection of North Korean college students in Bulgaria 202
1962: The year North Korea closed its doors 206

CHAPTER 5 From Stalin's children to Kim Il Sung's children
Kiss my younger brother Andrzej... 214
The moment of parting comes 219
Repatriation train 223
Kim Il Sung feared the children's return 226
Meeting a North Korean war orphan in Pyongyang 230
A last message to a friend in North Korea 233
Letters from North Korea 236
There is no hometown in the world that one cannot return to 242

Awards and Recognitions 245

About the Author 246

PROLOGUE

WHEN RECORDS DISAPPEAR, HISTORY IS ALSO FORGOTTEN

15 YEARS OF HISTORY TRACKING

In 1951, at the height of the Korean War, a train full of orphans left Pyongyang, the North Korean capital, and headed for the Trans-Siberian Railway. The children, who had lost their parents in the war and barely had enough food to eat, did not know where the train was taking them.

To transport hundreds of children at once, North Korean teachers even removed seats from the train cars. The children huddled together on the floors of the train cars and leaned against the sides of the rattling train. After 10 long days, the children arrived at their new homes.

From 1951 to 1953, special trains carried North Korean war orphans to cities in Poland, Romania, Bulgaria, Hungary, and Czechoslovakia. The official count of war orphans was over 5,000, but there was also an unofficial estimate of up to 10,000.

Why did North Korean children need to travel to Eastern Europe? And how did their carers manage to look after the kids there for as long as seven or eight years?

I spent 15 years tracing the history of the North Korean war orphans in Eastern Europe in order to learn the truth about this pivotal chapter in history. I then made a documentary film about it.

This book is a nonfiction account of the mass migration of North Korean war orphans to Eastern Europe during the Korean War.

A LOVE STORY ABOUT A WOMAN WHO TRANSCENDED BORDERS AND IDEOLOGIES

In 2004 I learned by chance about a woman in Romania who was waiting to be reunited with her North Korean husband. Her name was Georgeta Mircioiu, and she lived in the Romanian capital, Bucharest.

Her North Korean husband—the man she had waited for for over 40 years—was named Cho Chung Ho. He was a teacher who accompanied 3,000 North Korean war orphans to Romania in 1951.

During the Korean War, "Korea People's Schools" were established in Eastern European countries for North Korean orphans from the Korean War. Cho Chung Ho was the principal at one of the schools. This is how Georgeta Mircioiu, then a recent teachers' school graduate, first met Cho, then a 26-year-old North Korean.

A four-year secret international love affair, a marriage that had to be approved by the Romanian Communist Party, the repatriation of war orphans, and a relocation to Pyongyang in 1959 amid Eastern Europe's liberalization were all events that shook the life of this ordinary Romanian woman.

Through her life, I was able to learn about unfamiliar historical events such as the leadership challenge to North Korean leader Kim Il Sung, the clash with factionalists, and the exclusion campaign against foreign influence in North Korea in the 1960s.

More generally, learning about the migration of North Korean war orphans to Eastern Europe was also an opportunity to learn about North Korea's domestic history in the 1950s and 1960s.

In the early 1950s, 5,000 people boarded special trains from Pyongyang to Moscow and other Eastern European countries. In all, as many as 10,000 North Korean war orphans were brought to Eastern Europe. A photo of a special train for North Korean war orphans, discovered in Hungary during my first research trip.

In 2020, 16 years after learning of the story of Georgeta Mircioiu and Cho Chung Ho, I made a documentary film touching on the couple's love and fate, in the context of the history of the North Korean war orphans who lived in Eastern Europe.

The film, titled Kim Il Sung's Children, was first released in Korean cinemas. It was accepted by a well-known American distributor and was released worldwide on June 25, 2020, the 70th anniversary of the outbreak of the Korean War. It was screened at the International New York Film Festival in the United States and the Nice International

Film Festival in France.

Kim Il Sung's Children completely transformed my life as a writer and director.

Finding out about Mircioiu's life was fate, too. A documentary film director has a sense of obligation. That is why they take risks and search all over the world for hidden stories. The act of keeping a record is personal, but the record that is left is not.

It takes only a moment to leave a record, but that record can last for all time. If the record is lost, then the story may be lost as well. That is the sense of mission that documentary filmmakers have.

FINDING HIDDEN PIECES OF THE PUZZLE

Coincidentally, in the life of a Romanian woman waiting for her North Korean husband since they were separated in Pyongyang 60 years ago, the cult of personality surrounding Kim Il Sung, and North Korea's degeneration into a hermetically sealed political system, played a role.

I remember 15 years ago when I visited the National Film Archives in Romania to make a documentary about her. It was the first time I discovered a newsreel on the North Korean war orphans. The person in charge said she had spent days searching an old film warehouse for the canister.

As if coming out with an ossuary, she carefully brought out a silver film canister covered in dark rust. If someone hadn't set out to find them, the film canisters might have sat forever in the warehouse.

This was how we discovered the four-and-a-half-minute-long newsreel on the North Korean war orphans who came to Romania in 1953. While making this movie, I discovered about 100 photos and 50 letters sent by North Korean war orphans after their repatriation, not only in Romania but also in Poland, Bulgaria, the Czech Republic (established after the 1992 dissolution of Czechoslovakia), and Hungary.

Commemorative photo of North Korean war orphans found in the Czech Republic. This place was called "Kim Il Sung Academy."

The process of producing the documentary film Kim Il Sung's Children was a battle to find hidden records. Searching for unknown materials and piecing together the scattered records one by one was like assembling a puzzle. However, more difficult to find than the data were people still living in Eastern Europe who had taught or befriended North Korean orphans in the 1950s. There had been little documentation of them.

In the end, I was able to interview 12 of the orphans' living friends. Surprisingly, they remembered the names of the North Koreans they befriended in Europe 70 years ago. Some even remembered a song they sang with North Korean children. Their hearts were full of longing to see their friends again.

I would like to take this opportunity to once again express my gratitude to everyone who agreed to be interviewed. Without their testimony, this film could not have been made nearly as easily.

As we piece together this hidden history, the pieces that have already been found provide clues about the empty spaces that remain.

The last undiscovered piece of the puzzle in this story was the war orphans themselves. Unfortunately, in the course of my research, I was not able to meet even one of them. As a South Korean citizen, I obviously would not be allowed to enter North Korea easily, and even if I did, I would not be permitted to hunt for data from 70 years ago.

But more importantly, no one knows the ultimate fate of the war orphans who were repatriated to North Korea after living in Eastern Europe. No one outside North Korea can testify as to what happened to the children there or what kind of life they lived after returning there. All the children essentially disappeared.

The time will come when North Korea's closed society will open up, people in North and South Korea will be able to move freely throughout the peninsula, and the last missing piece of the puzzle will be revealed. Until then, I will not stop searching for the rest of the puzzle.

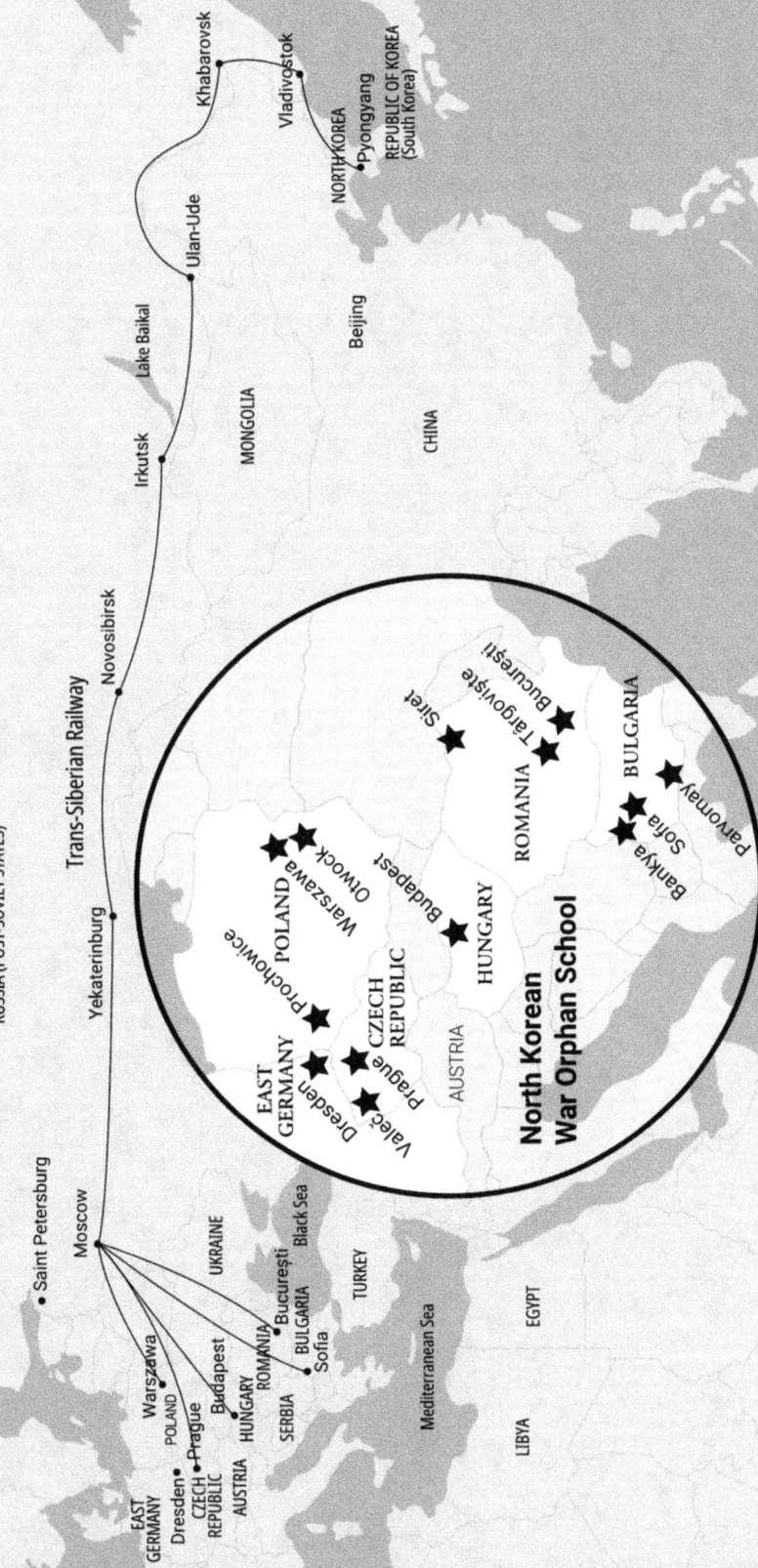

CHAPTER 1

CHILDREN FROM NORTH KOREA

TRACES OF NORTH KOREAN CHILDREN ACCIDENTALLY DISCOVERED

"Based on the Ministry of Foreign Affairs documents, that is, data sent from the Bulgarian embassies in Moscow, Beijing, and Pyongyang, there were at least 5,000 North Korean orphans who stayed in Eastern Europe from 1952 to around 1960—from 2,500 to 3,000 in Romania, 1,000 to 1,400 in Poland, 700 in Czechoslovakia, 500 in Hungary, and about 500 in Bulgaria."

— Jordan Baev, Bulgarian historian. From the movie Kim Il Sung's Children

On January 7, 2019, I took the train from Munich to my first destination, Regensburg, in eastern Germany. I was headed to meet Christophe Beckers and his wife, Kim Young-ja. Christophe Beckers was a German architect who, for several years, had been collecting data on North Korean orphans of the Korean War.

Because his wife was Korean, Beckers had a hobby of collecting any printed materials he found that had to do with Korea. While traveling in the Czech Republic, Beckers happened to see an intriguing article in a newspaper. It reported that at an old site in the Czech village of Valeč, on the side of an obelisk, the names of North Korean children had been discovered. That information was what prompted me to start researching the story of North Korean war

German architect discovers obelisk bearing the names of North Korean children

orphans.

Until 2004, the history of the North Korean war orphans who were housed in Eastern Europe remained hidden. Since most of this story took place in the 1950s, during the communist era, not many scholars studied it in depth after the countries of Eastern Europe underwent democratic transformations.

Key to uncovering this story were overseas Korean researchers—linguists specializing in Eastern European languages and literature. In recent years, they went to Eastern Europe to study. Soon after arriving, they heard that long ago, North Korean war orphans had been cared for in Eastern Europe. In most cases, they discovered this unexpectedly, while traveling in the region or studying diplomatic documents between North Korea and Eastern Europe in the 1950s.

It wasn't something I knew about.

"For my wife, who was living in an unfamiliar land, whenever an article or material containing the word 'Korea' came out, I automatically started collecting it. Then, one day, I happened to learn that an obelisk had an unfamiliar Korean name engraved on it. A few days later, I drove there myself and checked it out.
The names of two people are engraved on the side of the obelisk, which stands about seven meters high.
I took a picture and showed it to my Korean wife, and she said that the name was in the correct Korean order, with the surname first, followed by the given name.
That was the moment when I first discovered the traces of North Korean children."

— Christophe Beckers, German architect

Most of the traces of North Korean war orphans were found by chance. That was how Haeseong Lee, a professor of Korean language at the University of Wrocław, Poland, became aware of their story.

In 2007, Professor Lee drove to Prochowice, Poland, about 100 kilometers from Wrocław, to pick up his daughter from summer Bible school. Prochowice was German territory until the end of World War II, and German-style mansions still stood throughout the village. While walking among the old buildings, Professor Lee's eyes came across an inscription on the exterior wall of one.

When he looked at it closely, he was startled. The writing on the wall was in Korean. Moreover, it was in a distinctively North Korean style.

"From 1953 to 1959, we Korean War orphans studied at this school. We will never forget the warm and loving care of the people of Faran (Poland).
July 30, 1959. All orphans from Korea at the National Second Academy of Education."

Beckers (center) and local residents found an obelisk bearing the names of North Korean war orphans in Valeč, Czech Republic. From the movie Kim Il Sung's Children.

Professor Lee had not been aware that Eastern Europe had ever hosted North Korean war orphans. "Why would there be a Korean inscription on a building in a Polish village?" he wondered. He asked the villagers about the inscription. The villagers said it had been there for a long time, but no one knew its significance. Most of them didn't even know that it was in Korean.

From then on, Professor Lee sought out people who were researching the history of the village and started investigating. And he discovered the area's amazing history. In the 1950s, 1,400 North Korean war orphans had lived with Poles in the village of Prochowice.

"It's not a big city, and Prochowice was a rural town that was difficult to drive to. It was an amazing experience to find letters inscribed in Korean in such a place.
As I later found out, the date on the wall, 1959, was the year the North Korean children left.
From then on, whenever I had time, I collected data on the migration of North Korean children to Poland."

— Haeseong Lee, professor of Korean language, University of Wrocław, Poland

In Bulgaria, records of North Korean children studying at a Bulgarian school were discovered by a teacher who was cleaning out the school archives. In Hungary, at an orphanage on the outskirts of Budapest, someone remembered the playground where North Korean children played. In a school warehouse in Poland, a red insignia sent by a women's group affiliated with the Workers' Party of Korea as a token of appreciation was also found.

Otwock School, Poland, which houses records of the North Korean orphans (left)
A commemorative inscription on the exterior wall of the Prochowice State Central Secondary School in southwestern Poland (right)

Although the circumstances varied from country to country, generally, countries in Eastern Europe at the time tried to keep the North Korean children relatively isolated. In fact, most of the dormitories and schools selected for the children were in remote areas away from the big cities.

The authorities may have been worried that the local people would resent their facilities and resources being spent on war orphans from faraway North Korea. After all, in the 1950s, Eastern European countries were themselves still struggling to recover from World War II.

UNLOCKING SECRET DOCUMENTS

In the late 1990s, as secret documents were released following the collapse of the Soviet Union, new historical facts about the hosting of North Korean war orphans in Eastern Europe were revealed. The telegrams exchanged between communist parties and governments in Eastern Europe show that this initiative was carried out under the instructions of the Soviet Union.

Its purpose was to strengthen solidarity between socialist countries. At that time, the Soviet Union, the leader of the socialist bloc, met secretly with ambassadors from each country to determine how much assistance each country would provide.

Romania, which received the most war orphans—3,000—had among the most favorable economic conditions. However, most Eastern European countries were facing economic difficulties. Thus, the Soviets' plans for North Korean war orphans generated considerable friction with the communist governments of Eastern Europe. Bulgaria even sent a letter to Moscow stating that it could not accept the children.

Accommodating the war orphans meant providing them not only with accommodation but also with education and medical care. To complicate things, the host countries could not even predict how long the North Korean children would stay. According to the agreement, the children were to return to North Korea as soon as the

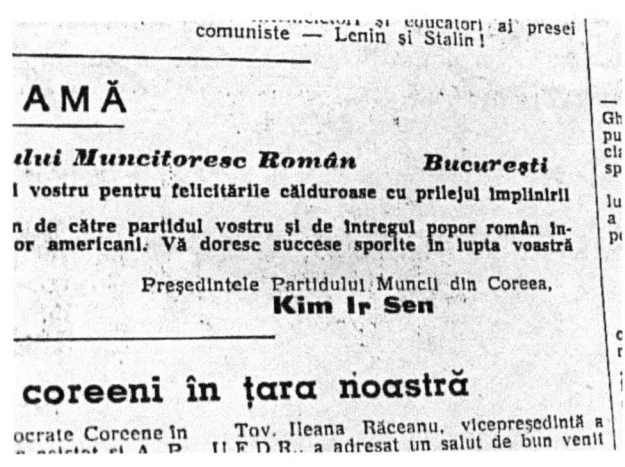

Kim Il Sung's message of appreciation, published in the official newspaper of the Communist Party of Romania. In Romanian, the name "Kim Il Sung" was pronounced and spelled "Kim Ir Sen."

economic condition there improved. In practice, however, sending the children back was not so straightforward.

Taking care of hundreds or thousands of children while providing free food, clothing and shelter for a long period of time was not an easy task.

Sending North Korean war orphans to Eastern Europe addressed the problem of how to care for them while, at the same time, reinforcing the leadership of the Soviet Union.

Inside North Korea, the political machinations of Kim Il Sung, the country's founder, also played a role. One article found in Romania indicates that Kim sent a telegram to the Romanian government containing a message of appreciation. Such materials show that North Korea intended to use the war orphans to strengthen diplomatic relations with Eastern Europe.

Eventually, these political and diplomatic interests were intertwined, and the relocation of North Korean war orphans to Eastern Europe progressed quickly. However, in practice, the project that offered little benefit to the countries in Eastern Europe.

This was why, in the early days of the project, telegrams were sent to Moscow from all over the world saying, "North Korean children cannot be accommodated."

The Soviet Union continued to push Eastern European countries to take in North Korean war orphans through the carrot of economic support and the stick of military pressure.

PHOTO ALBUM OF HIDDEN HISTORY

Inspired by finding the names of two children carved on an obelisk in Valeč in the Czech Republic, Beckers continued to look into the history of the North Korean war orphans. And in the process, he got to know a Czech woman who had once taken care of North Korean children. Her name was Marie Kopecká.

Kopecká and the North Korean children bonded with each other. Since the children could not speak Czech, she started learning Korean. The North Korean children, who initially thought of her as a stranger, gradually opened their hearts to her.

By the time the children returned to North Korea in 1956, an almost familial relationship had already formed between Kopecká and them. For Kopecká, the sudden repatriation of North Korean children was no small shock. That was why Kopecká began to record the deeds of North Korean children. After the children returned to North Korea, Kopecká was unable to reunite with them.

Meanwhile, 60 years passed. Kopecká grew old and frail. There was no further contact from the children who went to North Korea. However, her memories of the North Korean children did not disappear quickly.

By the time Beckers met her, Kopecká was in her mid-80s, suffering dementia, and living in a nursing home.

Marie Kopecká (second from left) and nursery teachers at Kim Il Sung Academy in Valeč, Czechoslovakia.

One day in 2017, Beckers received a phone call from Kopecká. She asked him to come to the nursing home. Kopecká knew she did not have much time left. She had a message to convey to the world. It was the story of the North Korean war orphans she had cared for. She handed Beckers a small cardboard box that she had cherished all her life.

"I hope someone will keep the things in this box.
I want someone to remember these things."

That was Kopecká's last request. Now, she was growing weak. She could no longer keep her mementos, but she didn't want the memories to disappear with her death. To her, they were irreplaceable.

Beckers opened the box. It was filled with photos of, and letters from, North Korean children. There was also a notebook in which Kopecká practiced writing Korean so she could write letters to the children.

There was also a photo album that she had put together. Between the photos, Kopecká had drawn in crayon pictures of flowers, trees, and the trains the children had arrived on.

Next to each photo, Kopecká had written the child's name in Korean. Her photo album, which covered the years 1952 to 1956, was a remarkable document recorded by an ordinary individual. As he turned each page in the album, Beckers could feel her sincere good will.

The children in the photos looked calm. Their faces were so bright that it was hard to believe that they had lost their parents in the war and had arrived in a distant, unfamiliar place. And there was a picture of Kopecká, smiling, standing next to the children. In the photo, they all look so peaceful and beautiful.

Beckers left the nursing home with Kopecká's box full of letters and her photo album. It was the last time the two met. Some might have considered the photo album nothing special, but it told a story of heartfelt friendship and affection. It was a historical record

Marie Kopecká's photo album contains pictures of North Korean children who stayed in Czechoslovakia in 1955.

compiled by an ordinary person.

Beckers started collecting data on North Korean war orphans in earnest. As a result, he learned that about 200 North Korean children had lived in Dresden, in what was then East Germany.

In Regensburg, Germany, I captured on camera the photo album of Kopecká's that Beckers kept. Her photo album was the first historical document he encountered when he began to research the history of North Korean children in Eastern Europe. The photos were in better condition than I expected.

The letters Kopecká wrote and the ones she received from the children in North Korea were, surprisingly, written in Czech. This demonstrated that the children had stayed in what was then Czechoslovakia long enough to learn Czech fluently.

The few letters from the children that were written in Korean contained many misspellings, and the Korean characters were poorly formed. By contrast, the children's letters in Czech were penned in perfect cursive.

REASONS WHY WE NEED A MIRACLE

When I saw the photo album, I wanted to go immediately to the Czech village where Kopecká met and lived with her children. What happened between the North Korean children and the European woman in that small world? I immediately started preparing my visit to the Czech Republic.

Initially the journey did not go smoothly. Heavy snow began to fall in the Regensburg region. Even so, we had to keep to our research schedule. Our destination was the rural Czech town of Valeč. It was the very place where the North Korean children in Kopecká's photo album stayed. It is approximately 200 kilometers from Regensburg to Valeč, and to get there, you have to cross Germany's eastern border. The area is in the Bohemian Forest. A minor road through a dense coniferous forest connects the German and Czech borders. Heavy snow had blocked roads throughout the area; in some places, people were trapped by it. Several car accidents had occurred.

Fortunately, the snow had stopped falling as I took the highway from Regensburg to the Czech border. A blue sky peeked through the dark clouds. I felt as if God were paving the way for my journey.

During the three months I spent traveling in Europe to make this documentary, miraculous things continued to happen. On my first day in Romania, I was about to cross the road at a crosswalk when a stranger approached me. He said in English: "If I say something like this, how will you respond?" Then he said "Hello" in Korean.

Since there are people everywhere who are curious about strangers, I thought this Romanian man just wanted to talk to a foreigner. In Eastern Europe, there weren't many Asians on the street, so I just thought he was curious about me, and I tried to move on. I simply answered the man and directed his attention towards the traffic light.

Suddenly, he brought up a story about his mother. "Actually, my mother had one very close friend. He was kind of special. My mother would always tell me the story of that friend.

"She said that she wanted to see him, and she was so sad that she couldn't ever meet him again. He looked just like you. He was a North Korean war orphan who came to Romania in the early 1950s and lived here. He went to the same school as my mother."

As soon as I heard the man's words, I groaned in disbelief. "I beg your pardon! A North Korean war orphan. Is that really true?!"

"Sure. I have a picture of my mother—can I show you?"

The man took an old black-and-white photo from his wallet and held it out for me to see. It was a picture of him and his mother, taken when he was young. I hadn't said a single word to him about my research of North Korean war orphans. What were the chances of meeting a Romanian man on the street who wanted to find a North Korean war orphan who was his mother's childhood friend?

I explained to him why I came to Romania. I told him that I was making a documentary about North Korean orphans in the Korean War.

Now it was the man's turn to be surprised. "No! How could there be such a coincidence? Actually, I had a meeting after work today; I usually don't go this way when I go home. But today, strangely, I took a different route and was walking on the road where I met you."

He considered it a very special coincidence. He didn't know I was making a documentary on North Korean war orphans until I told him. We exchanged contact information and agreed to get in touch

The Bohemian Forest straddles the German-Czech border.

if there were another opportunity in the future.

Meetings and separations of people often hinge on coincidences. Likewise, lifelong friendships and relationships with loved ones can start from very small coincidences. Meeting this Romanian man must have been such a coincidence. However, when coincidence goes beyond the everyday, those involved are bound to give meaning to that encounter.

This dramatic meeting with a man whose mother befriended a North Korean war orphan left a deep impression on me.

"If God is real, is he looking at our path now? Is he empowering us through this one-in-a-million coincidence?"

When I got home, I found that the man had contacted me on Facebook Messenger to say: "The moment was an amazing SIGN that there is a God. God bless your journey."

When we began our research in Eastern Europe, it was as if we were looking for a needle in a haystack. We were short on resources. I started off by funding the project out of my own pocket, without receiving support from any organization.

Nevertheless, I was highly motivated to go on a research trip in early January 2019 because I knew that the longer we waited, the more difficult it would be to find living associates of the war orphans.

Seventy years have already passed since the Korean War broke out. The historical material has gathered dust, and those in Eastern Europe who had befriended the North Korean war orphans have also grown older. More and more of them were dying.

In retrospect, I think I was able to complete the interviews thanks to such small miracles and inexplicable coincidences. At times when I couldn't even figure out who to meet or where to go, those strange experiences gave me the strength to continue. "Keep walking forward," it felt like someone was whispering to us. These little miracles exerted their power whenever I was ready to give up. Every time I lost strength in my legs, I felt as if someone was pushing me forward.

About an hour after we left Regensburg, our car reached the German-Czech border. As we crossed the border, the whole landscape was covered in snow. On both sides of the road through the woods were large piles of snow, placed there by snowplows. I thought about how difficult it would have been to drive down this road had the heavy snow not stopped.

After we drove for another 10 minutes, a huge coniferous forest appeared on both sides of us, like a folding screen. This was the Bohemian Forest. The snow-covered forest became more mysterious as we entered it. A world full of snow unfolded between the towering trees and the straight roads. We passed through and reached the Czech border.

There are no border checks between European Union countries today. However, before the establishment of the EU, those trying to enter Germany had to go through a border checkpoint. After a while, large clothing stores and shopping centers appeared.

Until the 1990s, South Vietnamese people who fled their country after the Vietnam War lived near x border. They mainly sold miscellaneous goods and daily necessities, and many of them immigrated to Germany illegally and traded. The Czech police did not stop this border trade, probably because they were able to earn a lot of money in kickbacks.

South Vietnamese people who fled Vietnam were known as "boat people." They risked their lives to flee from communist Vietnam by boat. There were up to 400,000 of them.

Most of their boats had no motors, so they drifted with the tides. Some boat people were lucky enough to reach refugee camps such as those in Singapore and Hong Kong, but many died at sea due to high winds or running out of drinking water. Some were even rescued by Australia as they drifted on the open seas. This meant that they drifted 2,000 kilometers from Vietnam to Australia. Some of those who survived emigrated to Europe and settled in the Bohemian Forest.

The sad history in the Bohemian Forest made my heart sink. Until we came out of the forest, the Vietnamese refugees who risked their lives to escape did not leave my mind. Before the Czech Republic joined the European Union, long lines of vehicles formed here to go through border controls to enter Germany. Reportedly, it was common to see street prostitutes soliciting here. Often, what lies behind such sudden appearances of people is sheer desperation.

There are no longer border controls between Germany and the Czech Republic. Because the border controls disappeared, the Vietnamese refugees and the prostitutes who smiled at strangers have long since disappeared. Compared to the past, when patrolled borders separated countries and people's lives and cultures changed along those borders, the current borders of Europe are just faint lines on a map. Thus, it is harder to find identifiable traces of the past now. Time has overshadowed everything.

Suddenly, from the car window, soaring roofs, like spires, came into view. Most of them were all-black roofs. The spires evoked the well-known Church of Our Lady of Tyn in Prague. As the sun went down, the two pointed spires, bathed in the sunset light, looked even more eerie in the cold winter weather. On the road, signs in Czech began to appear. Finally, we entered the Czech Republic. As we went further, the road became narrower and narrower, and the traffic became much lighter.

There was only one road to Valeč. Some stretches of it are so narrow that if you meet a car heading in the opposite direction, you need to pull off to the shoulder to let the other car pass. Around 1953, North Korean war orphans must have come down this road as well.

Church of Our Lady of Tyn in Prague.

After we passed through the forest and crossed the river, the plains of Valeč spread out before us, and a village was nestled in the middle of the plain. Finally, we arrived at our destination, the Czech village of Valeč.

> "The children came from faraway East Asia. They had different faces and used different words. They came to the remote Czech countryside, freed from fear and the horrors of war.
> At first, even in Czechoslovakia, the children were not welcome. Their existence was kept strictly secret. Hidden in the forest like a fairytale village, the children had to live in secret, with their backs to the world."
> — Christophe Beckers, German architect

NORTH KOREAN CHILDREN'S DORMITORY, VALEČ CASTLE

Valeč is a small rural town of 640 people located 100 kilometers west of Prague, the Czech capital. In this area, once known as the Sudetenland, Germans and Czechs had lived together since ancient times. This is why German-style houses and culture remain in the Valeč area.

In 1938, Nazi Germany forcibly annexed western Czechoslovakia on the grounds that it had been settled by Germans. However, as World War II ended with an Allied victory, defeated Germany had to assume responsibility for the war and cede the Valeč region back to Czechoslovakia. Thus, the village of Valeč changed hands several times.

The first thing I noticed at the entrance to the village was a large obelisk. Obelisks were typically erected in ancient Egypt to commemorate a war victory or to celebrate the achievements of a pharaoh. I did not expect to see one in a small village in the Czech Republic.

In Europe, there is a tradition of erecting an obelisk near a Baroque building. The obelisk served as a border marker between villages and as a landmark. It was located in a place that could be seen from anywhere in Valeč. There are still Baroque buildings scattered throughout Valeč, such as Valeč Castle.

Built around 1727, Valeč Castle seems altogether too big for the village it sits in. It was home to German aristocrats. During World War II, it was temporarily used as a sanatorium for the wounded. After World War II, the German aristocracy was expelled. In 1976, a major fire broke out in Valeč Castle, and the roof collapsed. Today, Valeč Castle is the property of the Czech government.

According to the records, about 100 orphans from the Korean War lived there from 1952 to 1956. Valeč Castle was provided to them by the Czech communist government. It was about 40 kilometers from the resort town of Karlovy Vary, famous for its hot springs, yet it was not well known to the outside world. It was the perfect place to accommodate children from North Korea.

Not only in Czechoslovakia but also elsewhere in Eastern Europe, the dormitories for North Korean war orphans were set up in places isolated from the outside world.

In Bulgaria, the records show that the children commuted about an hour to school in the capital, Sofia, from the city of Bankya, a resort town for the wealthy. At this time, the Bulgarian government provided the children with an entire hotel, containing more than 80 rooms.

Starting around 1955—three or four years after they came to Eastern Europe—the children were dispersed into isolated rural villages where large numbers of people were accommodated and metropolitan areas with a small number of elites. As time went on, children who had grown older and had to go into higher education, as well as the most academically gifted children, mostly migrated to local schools near large cities. These include Otwock, near Warsaw, Poland; Târgoviște, near Bucharest, Romania; and Bankya, Bulgaria.

In Hungary, a small number of children lived in a place on the outskirts of the capital, Budapest. North Korean children were taught in the same classrooms as Hungarian children. Schools and dormitories in metropolitan areas where the North Korean children stayed appeared in communist propaganda newsreels.

A Baroque castle in Valeč, Czech Republic, where North Korean children lived in the early 1950s.

There are also many staged scenes of the war orphans in newsreels and photographs from that time. Some children from North Korea gave exaggerated performances, as if they were playing the lead in a movie. It was interesting to see the children, who had lost their parents in the war and fell into despair, shout slogans about building a socialist country.

The humanitarian project of accepting North Korean war orphans was actually a propaganda tactic to promote and reinforce socialist ideology.

"You have to remember that it was the 1950s.
The Soviets wanted to expand their influence around
the world somehow. A symbolic act was needed to show
that Eastern European countries were superior to Western
European ones and to demonstrate socialist solidarity and

internationalism.
Children from the country where the Korean War took place were so special. A propaganda campaign called on other communist countries to help and share
the suffering of the communist state fighting the U.S. imperialists."

— Jolanta Krysowata, Polish documentary director

THE FIRST IMPRESSIONS

When I met and interviewed people in Eastern Europe who had known the North Korean orphans, I was especially curious about their first impressions of the children. Though 60 years had passed, they remembered everything from the moment they first met the children to the moment they parted. Some remembered the children's ages, names, faces, and even the story of the last time they saw them.

> "The children came by train. I remember it was the winter of 1952. All the Bulgarian students went to the station to welcome the North Korean children. It snowed very heavily that day."
> — Kata Panelutova, Bulgarian classmate of North Korean war orphans

> "I still remember the scene where the children got off the train. Everyone was in clean clothes. I heard later that they all changed into uniforms in the Soviet Union."
> — Petrov Kolev, Bulgarian classmate of North Korean war orphans

> "It was difficult to have a conversation at first. We communicated through gestures. Afterwards, we spent a lot of time together, so it wasn't too hard, and we

attended events together. There is one thing I remember. A war orphan boy I was studying with had appendicitis and was hospitalized. My younger sister was sick at the same time and was hospitalized in the same room. My mother took care of my sister in the same room, but the North Korean boy couldn't communicate well, so my mother must have helped him. So he really liked her. Even after he was discharged, he kept coming over to our house to play. He said that in North Korea, his parents were doctors, but they had both died. I still remember the name of that friend: Jeon Nak-won."

— Lilka Anatasova, Bulgarian classmate of North Korean war orphans

"From the first time I saw them, I thought they were well-mannered children. And just as they looked at us with curiosity, we looked the same way at them. After that, we became very close. But what surprised me the most was the North Korean students' attitude.
Even though life was really hard in North Korea, they seemed calm. They always worked enthusiastically, whether playing together or in class. They were well-prepared students and really wanted to learn."

— Lilka Anatasova

Halina Dovek, a teacher who taught North Korean children in Poland, recalled that many children had trouble adjusting to the local food when they first arrived. However, after a year or so, the children were fully accustomed to European food. Instead of rice, they began to enjoy foods such as cheese and macaroni, and some children even made kimchi (Korean fermented cabbage) themselves.

"The children's house didn't have anything special to eat. At that time, even in Poland, goods were not so abundant.

Bulgarian students went to the station just in time for the train to welcome children from faraway North Korea.

The children grew vegetables in the garden. Afterwards, they dug them out, mixed them up in their own way, and ate them. They made kimchi."

— Halina Dovek, Polish teacher of North Korean war orphans

"There was a class leader among the children. They were very disciplined. I still remember the words they used: ora, gara, and saekkiya. I remember that the word saekkiya meant a dog. It was a word that older students called younger students."

— Stanisław Wachal, Polish teacher of North Korean war orphans

All the still-living Eastern European friends or teachers of the North Korean children whom we managed to track down had surprisingly specific and accurate memories. In Bulgaria, one elderly man I interviewed was recalling old memories when suddenly, he began to sing.

> *"Bright traces of blood on the crags of Jangbaek still gleam,*
> *Still the Amnok carries along signs of blood in its stream.*
> *Still do those hallowed traces shine resplendently*
> *Over Korea ever flourishing and free.*
> *So dear to all our hearts is our General's glorious name,*
> *Our own beloved Kim Il Sung of undying fame."*
>
> (Translation: https://kkfonline.com/2020/05/05/song-of-general-kim-il-sung/)

The lyrics were all in Korean. It was a song he had sung with North Korean children. After the man finished the first verse, a few elderly women who were waiting to be interviewed approached the camera. They sang together. After the song was over, they shouted "Long live Kim Il Sung!"

At the time, I didn't know what song they were singing. Later, I checked and found out that it was "The Song of General Kim Il Sung." The lyrics praised Kim Il Sung's achievements. It was astonishing that elderly Bulgarians, who could not speak Korean at all, could accurately remember "The Song of General Kim Il Sung" even after 60 years.

> "I learned from them. It was a song that North Korean children sang almost every day.
> So I think we naturally memorized it in our heads."
>
> — Veselin Kolev, Bulgarian classmate of North Korean war orphans

Surprisingly, when "The Song of General Kim Il Sung" was written in 1947, it was during the unsettled period after liberation when the state and constitution were not yet properly established in either North or South Korea.

According to the testimony of defectors, in North Korea "The Song of General Kim Il Sung" is more important than the national anthem. This is further evidence of the intensity of Kim Il Sung's cult of personality.

The author interviewing Veselin Kolev, a Bulgarian classmate of North Korean war orphans, for the movie *Kim Il Sung's Children*. Bulgarian classmates of North Korean war orphans. (bottom picture).

    The North Korean children's old friends whom I met in Eastern Europe recalled that the North Korean children sang "The Song of General Kim Il Sung" every day during the morning assembly. This fact was confirmed in old documentary footage.

NORTH KOREAN CHILDREN'S REPORT CARDS

This investigation has unearthed previously unknown documents and sources. The personal records containing the North Korean children's names, hometowns, and other life details were a valuable resource. The children's school transcripts were included in these personal records. These give us an idea of how hard the children studied while in Eastern Europe. The children got high marks in most subjects, except for local languages. In math and science, they were far ahead of the European children.

> "This student's name was Ahn Hye-Geum. She was born on August 22, 1940, and her hometown was Cheongjin. She spoke Bulgarian quite well. She got (a mark of) four out of six in Bulgarian. It must have been an unfamiliar language, but she did well enough. She arrived in 1952 and stayed until 1959. Math, science, astronomy, history, geography, physical education, music, art—she did well in everything. The records also show that she skipped 10th grade because she had good marks."
>
> — Nikolai Nikolov, history teacher at School No. 36 in Parvomay, Bulgaria

From 112-year-old School No. 18 in Sofia, Bulgaria, to School No. 78 in Bankya, the children who adapted well moved to different schools. In Hungary, some children went to technical schools to learn coal-mining techniques or to get training in textile factories.

At that time, North Korea desperately needed coal-mining know-how. The children were supposed to learn advanced techniques from Eastern Europe so that in the future, they could serve as engineers in North Korea.

However, all these plans were canceled due to the winds of liberalization that blew in Eastern Europe in 1956. The rapidly changing situation in Eastern Europe led North Korea to suddenly order its children home.

Though the children had already lived in Europe for years, had made new friends and had what was like a foster family, they were fast approaching the moment when they would have to say goodbye. The children came from a war-torn land and adapted to survive in Europe. Their sudden repatriation meant another tragedy for the children.

In most Eastern European schools, finding the children's records was not easy after so many years. In the end, the only option was to go into the warehouse to find the documents, guided in part by the memories of the old teachers who worked at the school.

In Parvomay, Bulgaria, in the dusty warehouse containing the school's archives, Bulgarian teachers searched for the North Korean children's records for hours. They thumbed through hundreds of pages searching for the relevant names. The heating inside the warehouse was not working properly, so a bitter winter wind pierced the windows. If the teachers opened their mouths even a little to talk, their cold breaths hung in the air. If it had been someone else's project, I probably wouldn't even have come forward to help.

Despite these difficulties, the Bulgarian teachers never gave up looking for the documents. Once again, I would like to express my sincere gratitude to Nikolai Nikolov, teacher at School No. 36 in

Parvomay, Bulgaria, who braved all the difficulties to search for the records.

As silently watched the people who, even after 70 years, had kept the records of children who had been guests from faraway Korea, I felt great respect for them.

Nikolov, who had been leafing through the pile of documents, suddenly shouted that he had found something: the names of North Korean children, written in Cyrillic letters.

"It's all here. All the records of the North Korean children who studied at our school are here!"

Nikolov read the names of North Korean children one by one.

> "Go Dong-hyun, Cho Man-ki, Park Eun-cheon,
> Koo Dong-chil, Cha Myeong-sik, Park Gyu-ja,
> Jang Jin-seong, Son Kyeong-ja, Cheon Bong-ho,
> Ri Yeon-bok, Park Young-chan, Jang Seon-nam,
> Ri Jeong-yu, Kim Seong-man, Kwon Chan-il,
> Ri Sang-jong, Cho Kyung-choon, Yang Jin-cheol,
> Jeon Dae-sik, Kang Jung-woo, Kim Jong-seon,
> Kim Ju-nam, Kim Kyung-wha, Ahn Seon-hwa...."

The names of the children continued endlessly. The Bulgarian teacher grew quieter as he read the personal records with the children's names. His voice trembled.

"I've been looking for these for a long time. Here, the children's hometowns and birth dates are recorded. In the next column, can you see all the grades the children received? The children studied very hard. It wouldn't have been easy to go to a foreign country… The Bulgarian teacher wrote in the last column: 'This student can go on to the next grade.'… The homeroom teacher even co-signed it. This is really impressive."

"Kim Ki-yeon came in 1956 and entered the eighth grade and studied until 1958. There's no record after that. You can see that each

CHILDREN FROM NORTH KOREA   41

The school records of a North Korean war orphan found at School No. 18 in Sofia, Bulgaria.

History teacher Nikolai Nikolov found North Korean war orphans' personal records from the 1950s in the warehouse of School No. 36 in Parvomay, Bulgaria.

child stayed for a slightly different length of time. They came around 1952 and returned to North Korea between 1958 and 1959."

"Jang Sun-hwa received high marks in Bulgarian, Russian, and math. Six is the highest mark, so a mark of four or five is good. I see here that Korean is also a subject. This serves to confirm that we taught Korean separately. By the way, this student only got a mark of four in Korean. She was from Korea, so why couldn't she do well? She should have gotten a mark of six."

"This student's name was Ri Jeong-sang. His hometown was Cheonjin. He was born in 1940, so he came to Bulgaria when he was 15. There was also a column to indicate the parent's job. This student had a father, and it says he was a manual laborer. Ri Chan-sam seems to have been the student's father's name. How amazing. The fact that such records exist...."

"Most of the students are from the provinces, but this student, Kim Ju-nam, is recorded as being from Pyongyang. That is uncommon. He was born on November 17, 1942. He studied very well. I see that his grades were high in all subjects."

Records indicating that a few North Korean war orphans were from Pyongyang were also found at School No. 18 in Sofia, Bulgaria. It seemed likely that they were the children of high-ranking party officials.

There were also children whose hometown was in South Korea. In these cases, the children were orphaned when North Korea occupied Southern territory and were later evacuated to the North as the front line moved northward.

In Poland, there were even recollections that some of the North Korean war orphans had fathers.

"The fact that there were children with parents was an open secret at the time. Most likely, they were the children of high-ranking party leaders. One day, a child's father visited the school. According to the rules, he couldn't reveal himself as the child's biological father as his child was supposed to be an orphan, so he just went to see the child. It would be painful for other war orphans to learn that some of their classmates' parents were alive. Those parents and children had to pretend not to know each other and just glanced at each other's faces."

— Stanisław Wachal, Polish schoolteacher of North Korean war orphans

WAR TRAUMA

"North Korean orphans were suffering not only physically but also mentally. Because they were children who had witnessed war."
— Dmitry Kristoff, history teacher at School No. 78 in Bankya, Bulgaria

"Once, a fighter jet flew over a village as part of a military exercise. The North Korean children screamed and panicked. Trembling in fear, the children ran behind their teacher and held each other and hid. It must have been because of painful memories of the war."
— Boris Voyajeev, Bulgarian classmate of North Korean war orphans

The problem, however, is that the children had no one they could talk to about such trauma. They had to hide their pain, because the North Korean teachers and minders were closely observing them, and those children who were struggling psychologically were repatriated to North Korea.

However, the European teachers understood the feelings of these children better than anyone else. They deliberately took the children to the woods under the pretext of outdoor learning. They did so because in the woods, there was no need to obey the North Korean teachers.

Siret, Romania, North Korean war orphans. The European teachers would occasionally teach the children outside.

This allowed the children to experience firsthand the beauty of nature and the small joys of everyday life. It allowed the children to enjoy the freedom they could not feel in the classroom.

> "If you went to the forest with the children, as soon as the minders from North Korea disappeared, the Polish teachers would announce to the children: 'Guys! Now you don't have to march in step with each other. You don't even need to look at the others. From now on, run and play to your heart's content! You are free!'"
> — Jolanta Krysowata, Polish documentary director

Most of the children learned the local language over time and were able to communicate openly with Eastern Europeans. They also learned Eastern European culture and ways of life. The younger the child, the faster he or she adapted to the new environment. The speed at which North Korean children learned the local language was astonishing.

Indeed, the children under the age of five, in many cases, forgot their native language and had difficulty writing Korean. Seven or eight years is a long period of time, enough to change the identity of children. As time passed, more and more children grew confused as to whether they were Korean or European.

For this reason, the North Korean authorities dispatched North Korean teachers to Europe to educate the children. However, as time passed, conflicts between European and North Korean teachers emerged. The roots of the conflicts lay in a difference in mindset—that is, between collectivism and individualism.

The education of the war orphans in Eastern Europe was coercive and group-oriented. The decisions about what the children would study and what their futures would be were all made by the North Korean ambassadors to Eastern Europe. Some of the children, for instance, wanted to become artists, but none of them were given the chance to choose their own path in life.

> "North Korean teachers provided instruction strictly and systematically. There was no such thing as a free choice based on what suited the individual. This also made it difficult for children to adapt. Like it or not, the children had to do what their teachers and administrators told them to do. North Korea's closed organizational culture was already being tested on European soil in the 1950s."
> — Sylwia Szyc, Polish researcher of North Korea

Eastern European culture is more individualistic, even in the context of a communist state. The rationalist way of thinking that shaped European modern civil society also developed from an individualistic philosophy. The problem was that the North Korean teachers' educational approach emphasized the group rather than the individual. This and the high degree of regimentation in the program caused frequent clashes with teachers in Europe.

Sylwia Szyc,
a Polish researcher of
North Korea.

When the North Korean war orphans first arrived in Europe, their North Korean teachers strictly forbade them from hugging or otherwise showing affection to European teachers. Supposedly, the North Korean teachers were concerned that physical contact with the children or expressions of affection could make them weak. The Eastern European teachers found such a claim absurd and inhumane. How can you stop people from showing each other affection?

But the North Korean teachers had no intention of backing down. In their eyes, easing up even slightly meant potentially losing control of the children. In the early 1950s, confrontations between European and North Korean teachers took place often. In the end, it was decided to divide the roles. The North Korean teachers oversaw the children's ideological education. They taught the Korean language, history, and the worship of Kim Il Sung. The Eastern European teachers were in charge of teaching the arts, such as art and music.

The North Korean teachers were convinced that with this arrangement, they could take the lead in the children's education. What they did not expect was that the Eastern European teachers' arts education would transform the children's values.

Almost all Eastern European schools for North Korean war orphans had a strict hierarchy and surveillance system. For each group of 10 or so students, there was a class leader, and there was a

Professor Haeseong Lee, University of Wrocław, Poland.

leader who monitored them. Their lives were thoroughly organized and managed. No individual freedom was allowed. It was quite at odds with the relatively free atmosphere of Europe.

In the midst of this, some of the children naturally began to accept European-style liberalism. They also clashed with North Korean teachers during class. There were even some children who were skeptical of the indoctrination glorifying Kim Il Sung.

Later, when anti-Soviet resistance broke out in Eastern Europe in 1956, some of them joined it alongside Europeans.

Some children escaped from the dormitory and ran away, or applied for asylum at the French or American embassies.

How could these children become so rebellious when the North Korean teachers' educational approach was based on intense surveillance and collectivism? Seeking the answer to this question was the most interesting part of my research in Eastern Europe. For identifying which factors changed children's thinking and behavior back then would help us understand what might change North Korean society in the future.

In conclusion, it was art and culture that brought about this change in the children. In particular, the role of literature was enormous. As the children read ancient Greek mythology, classical literature, and Shakespeare under the tutelage of Eastern European teachers, they realized that there was a world completely different from the uniform collectivism emphasized by North Korean teachers. A few children even borrowed books to read secretly, out of sight of the North Korean teachers. What they discovered was introspection—the power to examine their own lives for themselves. The children's eyes were opened to the concepts of freedom and human rights that shaped Europe's modern civil society. This seismic shift would never have happened if the children had not lived in Eastern Europe.

Perhaps the two students whose names were carved on the side of the obelisk in Valeč—Lim Ki-jong and Byun Cheol-ho—were among those who woke up to this new idea. Their names could only have been carved using a sharp metal tool. Moreover, the obelisk would have been difficult for children to climb: it stands seven meters high, and the height from the ground to the base alone was about two meters.

Moreover, it would have taken a lot of time for the children, who had lived a strict communal existence, to come to the obelisk, far away from the dormitory, and carve their names on its surface. They had to sneak out of the dormitory to escape the teachers' surveillance.

So, in 1956, before leaving Valeč, which they were fond of, they tried to leave their mark somehow. Valeč was like their second hometown, and they knew they might never come back again.

The earnest wishes of the children were expressed on the side of the obelisk. It was the longing for freedom that only children who had tasted freedom could feel. The children's names carved into the stone had not disappeared, even after many years. Do they know that the name they carved in 1956 is still there? I stood on the windswept hill where the obelisk stood and softly called their names. "Lim Ki-jong…. Byun Cheol-ho…."

ANGEL ON THE ROAD: MARIE KOPECKÁ

We entered Valeč Castle under the guidance of the staff of the Valeč Archives. Built in the 18th century, the Baroque-style Valeč Castle was grander inside than I expected. It is a five-story building with 40 rooms.

Inside were sculptures and murals depicting heroes from Greek mythology. The guide explained that the building now functions as a gallery displaying the works of local artists.

I passed the large hall on the first floor and went up the marble stairs. A large hall is located in the center of each floor, and passing through the hall takes you to a hallway, with rooms on either side.

The size of one room was only about 10 square meters. Each room had a large window, so there was a lot of light. When I opened the window, I saw that there was a small balcony outside. As I stood on the balcony, I could see the panoramic view of Valeč in the distance. All of a sudden, flurries of snow chilled me. The wind was so strong that I could not continue standing on the balcony.

The roughly 100 North Korean war orphans who migrated to Valeč typically lived four to a room. It was not a large space for children to live in, but it was enough for children who had lost everything in war.

Documents about the children from North Korea were kept in the archives of Karlovy Vary, the administrative district to which the

Maria Kopecika, who took care of North Korean children in Valeč, Czech Republic, right before she contracted dementia (left).

village of Valeč belonged.

Beckers, the German researcher in Regensburg, has visited the Karlovy Vary archives for the past five years to collect data on the North Korean children. Among the documents were the academic records and personal records of North Korean children. These were valuable materials that give us a more concrete picture of the lives of North Korean children who were staying in Valeč.

Among the materials Beckers kept, the most striking were the letters the children sent after they returned to North Korea. The children spoke Czech fluently because they had lived in Czechoslovakia for a long time. After returning to the North in 1956, the children carefully wrote letters in Czech and mailed them to Valeč.

Interestingly, the children's letters were addressed mainly to one person: Marie Kopecká, who was known as the "Angel on the Road" in Valeč.

Marie Kopecká had a fascinating life trajectory. She had a great interest in other cultures, which led her to travel to Africa and even to live in Morocco for several years. After returning to Czechoslovakia

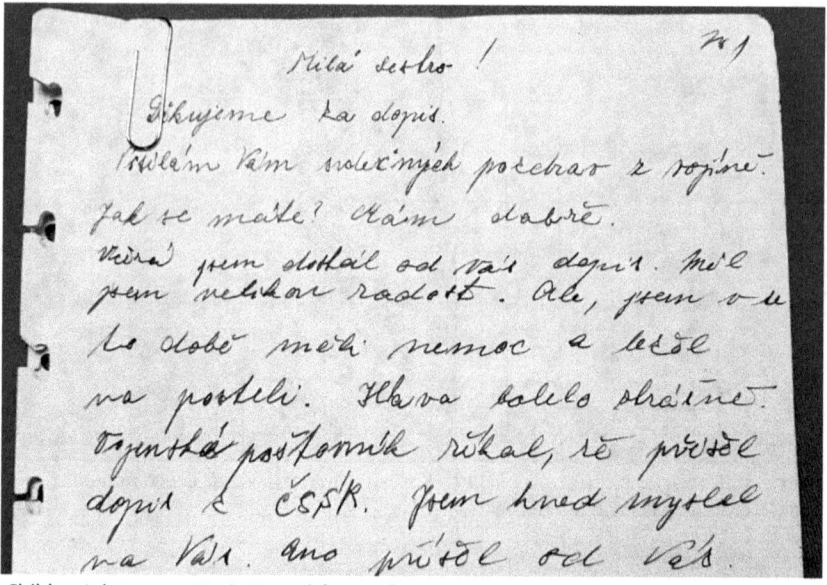

Children's letters to Marie Kopecká, sent from North Korea (1958).

in the late 1940s, she worked as a professor teaching geometry and mechanics at the University of Prague.

During the Korean War, Czechoslovakia sent medical personnel to North Korea as a form of socialist solidarity. At that time, the Czechs lionized North Korea for fighting on behalf of the socialist countries against the United States, which led the capitalist world.

Kopecká was intrigued by the North Korean war orphans who arrived in Czechoslovakia. She cherished socialist ideals, and she sympathized with the children who lost their parents in the tragedy of war and were all alone. Thus, Kopecká volunteered to help the orphans.

"The first time I met the kids was on our first summer vacation after college. I'm not sure if my memory is correct. I think it was 1952–1953. That was the year I first met the children. We often went to play near Valeč during summer vacation."

— Marie Kopecká

I remember the moment when I filmed Kopecká's photo album and letters from North Korean children. There was so much material that it took two full days to shoot, and it was of great value as historical material. As I captured the materials she had left behind on camera, it felt like I was meeting a noble soul.

Among the materials, there was also a notebook for the study of Korean; Korean characters were sparsely interspersed between notes in Czech. This was evidence that Kopecká had studied Korean in order to communicate with the North Korean children.

What did the North Korean war orphans mean to this Czech woman? I wondered what kind of friendship blossomed between them 70 years ago.

She had written the names of the children in Korean, next to their pictures. Perhaps it was because after the children left, she did not want to forget who was who. After being sent back to North Korea, the children exchanged letters with Kopecká until around 1958.

In the letters, the children called Kopecká their "sister." They were very friendly.

"To my sister, Marie Kopecká.... Over time, we are also getting older. Now we are undergoing various kinds of military training. If you score high, you can receive a medal and finish your training. To earn that honor, we study hard every day. There is also a lot to study. "This is my first year in middle school. When we graduate from school, our lives will be better."

— A letter from North Korea

Even after returning to North Korea, the children each tried to tell Kopecká about their life there. Their letters were written with tenderness, as if they had been whispered right next to her. Perhaps it was because of the personal connection between students and teacher, amplified by the tragedy of war. Thus, Kopecká still treasured the letters 70 years later.

WHEN RECORDS DISAPPEAR, HISTORY IS FORGOTTEN

I tried to contact Marie Kopecká through various channels, but unfortunately, she was not able to meet me. Due to dementia, she could no longer recognize her family and was so frail that she could not get out of bed by herself. Everyday records are sometimes seen as more important than the grandiose interpretations of historians. Such were the records of Kopecká.

During the day, I interviewed and filmed people, and in the evening I returned to the dormitory to carefully photograph Kopecká's photo album and letters. Shooting the photo album took me until dawn. None of it could be left out. I thought that this might turn out to be the only remaining documentation of North Korean war orphans in the Czech Republic.

What moved me more than anything else was the children's innocent and bright expressions in the photos. In parks and playgrounds, they stood together like siblings. In their bright faces, there was heartfelt human affection.

Kim Jang-jin, Park Kyung-bo, Park In-dok,
Hong Jun-soon, Shin Young-pil, Ri Su-ja, Ko Jae-jeong,
Kim Yu-soon, Kim Ki-bo, Shin Dong-seon,
Lim Gyeong-hwan, Kang Ki-chan, Yang Moon-hee,

North Korean children appearing in Marie Kopecká's photo album.

Ko Je-jeong, Bae Bong-hak, Choi Si-yeol, Jeong Bo-bae, and Ko Jong-ok....

Kopecká had written the children's names in Korean next to their pictures. Thus, we were able to identify them. Although there was no way to ascertain whether they were now alive or dead, finding their names and images was a real breakthrough. In the future, if there is an opportunity, with North Korea's cooperation, to identify them, these names and photos can serve as a starting point.

Most of the war orphans were born in the early 1940s and were around 10 years old in 1950, during the Korean War. Since 70 years have passed since then, they would now be about 80 years old. Some of them could still be alive today. Perhaps we will be able to track them down someday.

But at present, there is no way for us to know what became of them. The children from North Korea disappeared as suddenly as they had come. At the teacher's command, everyone lined up and got off the train, and when they had to go back, they lined up again and got on the train.

They took the Trans-Siberian Railway on a 10-day train journey back to North Korea. They had lived under European skies long enough for the boys to start sprouting mustaches and the girls to grow into women. It was only natural that they were missed by their European teachers and classmates.

The children who returned to North Korea wrote letters in Czech to Marie Kopecká.

"To my sister, who I want to see. Thank you for the letter.
Right now, as I reply to your letter, I'm in the military.
Are you doing well? I got your letter yesterday.
I was really happy. Actually, I had a bit of a headache at that time and was lying down. As soon as the delivery man told me that a letter had arrived from Czechoslovakia by military mail, I thought, 'Could that be a letter from you?' Then I got your letter. As soon as I received the letter, I opened the envelope and read it. It was so nice and I was so happy. A friend who was next to me looked at the writing on the letter and said, 'What's wrong with the writing?' and laughed. It was the first time he had seen Czech handwriting. We laughed together for a long time. Then I told him, 'I mean.... I can read this letter!'
Sister! A few days ago, I bought a painting of a tiger. I'm going to send it to you. My comrade commander of our unit said he would help me send the painting to Czechoslovakia.
I hope the painting will get there soon. I'm done for today. Can you send me a picture of yourself too?"

— A letter from North Korea

The names of North Korean children are carved into an obelisk in the Czech village of Valeč. Even today, the inscriptions "Lim Ki-jong," "Byun Cheol-ho," and "1956" are clearly visible.

My eyes lingered on this letter longer than any other. I could feel the real connection between the war orphans and Kopecká. After returning to North Korea, the children waited for her letters; there was no letter that recorded their feelings more earnestly than this one. Even now, I can imagine a young man in North Korea showing a friend the letter he got from Kopecká, written in Czech, and bragging, "I can read this letter."

Starting around 1959, letters from the children to Kopecká stopped coming. North Korean authorities were intercepting the letters, as they contained stories that the regime did not want the outside world to know. Kopecká's last remaining contact with the children was broken. But their impact on her was indelible. Just before she contracted dementia, Kopecká wrote to the world.

Marie Kopecká and the North Korean children sometimes went on excursions together.

"I am so happy that my children have had an enjoyable and wonderful life in Valeč. I worked part-time in a nursery where my children were staying. The children looked very happy back then. There were over a hundred children there.
Valeč Castle was provided for them to live in. We did our best to teach and care for the children. All the teachers from North Korea were great. We later learned that Kim Il Sung was the only one who was not happy with this situation. Because there was a fear that the children would return to North Korea influenced by Western culture."

Even the teachers from North Korea who were in charge of children's ideological education and language education were satisfied with their life in Europe. The Europeans who took care of the children were also happy. As Marie Kopecká's testimony indicates, the only dissatisfied person was Kim Il Sung. While friendships and encounters were formed between ordinary people, Kim thought only of his own political ends.

That is why Kopecká turned against Kim Il Sung after the children returned to North Korea. And this did not just happen in Czechoslovakia. In all the relevant countries, including Poland, Romania, Bulgaria, and Hungary, Eastern Europeans expressed antipathy towards the North Korean regime.

Jolanta Krysowata, who directed the documentary Kim Ki Dok (2006), about the lives of North Korean orphans in Poland, explains this as follows.

> "It was only five or six years after the end of World War II. There was also a shortage of doctors for Poles all over Poland, because a lot of medical school professors had died.
> Nevertheless, Poland sent envoys to North Korea. The reason that Poland lacked doctors was because they were sent to North Korea first, based on the propaganda that other communist countries should help and share in the suffering of communist countries fighting against the United States. This was politics and propaganda—I mean it, propaganda—until average ordinary Poles met the children from North Korea. The Polish people who met with North Korean children at the time were really young. So young Poles aged 17–19 met North Korean children, and Polish children also met North Korean children. From that moment on, this contact began to turn into love and friendship."

— Jolanta Krysowata, documentary director

The orphans were able to overcome the pain of the past because they were surrounded by kind-hearted people like Marie Kopecká, who cared for them without asking for anything in return.

It didn't just happen in the small rural town of Valeč. In Poland, Romania, Bulgaria, and Hungary, there were also people who warmly welcomed the North Korean children. The children followed these carers as if they were their own parents. To the children, these people were angels they met on the road.

On January 12, 2019, I had to leave the Czech Republic to travel to my next destination. As I was packing, I kept thinking of Marie Kopecká and the children. The memories of the rural village of Valeč remain in my heart. They were people I could only get to know by name and photo, but they must have had remarkable lives.

Kopecká did not receive any compensation. She never anticipated a reward. She cared for the North Korean orphans without any self-interest. If she hadn't recorded her memories, her existence would have been forgotten with time.

Fortunately, the photo album she put together and the letters she exchanged with her students are now preserved as valuable historical documents. I hope that, through my documentary film Kim Il Sung's Children, she will always be remembered.

I WANT TO GO BACK
TO MY EUROPEAN HOME

I was often surprised at what their European friends told me about the North Korean children's thoughts and actions. Many episodes that occurred right before the children's sudden repatriation to North Korea in 1956 suggest how kind-hearted they were.

North Korean children and their European teachers and friends alike could hardly believe that they had to tell each other goodbye. For them, parting was unimaginable. They believed they would be living together for a long time, like family or friends. The children's behavior just after their repatriation to North Korea was announced suggests how much they regretted having to leave.

> "The children were very sad when they heard that they were going back to the North. The night before they left, I saw a child in a cold snow pit, rolling back and forth in the snow while undressed. This young child's behavior was so strange that I asked him, 'Why are you doing this?' The child's response was surprising: 'If I catch a cold this way, I may not have to board the train tomorrow.'"
> — Marie Kopecká

Because the children had lived in Eastern Europe for years, they were able to speak the local language fluently. Thus, after returning to North Korea, the children exchanged correspondence with their teachers and friends in Eastern Europe. The children needed someone to confide in about their new environment and their uncertain future.

From 1956 to 1958, these letters went freely between North Korea and Europe. The problem was that the children's letters included descriptions of the difficult economic situation inside North Korea or requests for basic necessities. A few children even begged, "I want to come home"—meaning back to Eastern Europe. These letters were regarded as unacceptable by the North Korean authorities. Thus North Korea conducted extensive mail censorship. By 1959, such correspondence was completely blocked.

> "Greetings to our teacher. How are you today? These days, I am picking cherries in the mountains and cooking them. We share them with children. They are all good and fun kids. One of my wishes is to have paper on which to write letters. I wish I had something like a small diary. I am waiting for your letter.
>
> "Mom! I miss you.
> Please send me some clothes.
> I want to go back home."

Because they had lost their parents in the war, the children had no one left in North Korea with whom they could talk openly. In addition, life in North Korea, which was economically backward, could not satisfy children who had experienced the relatively advanced life and culture of Eastern Europe. That was why the children wrote and asked for material things that they lacked. As a result, the outside world became more aware of the problems of the

North Korean war orphans living in Prochowice, Poland, 1958.

North Korean system.

> "In Poland, correspondence began to cease in 1959. Before then, there was some exchange of letters. Politically, 1959 was a time when North Korea was minimizing relations and exchanges with all foreign countries. Even North Korean diplomats posted abroad were banned from talking to locals without permission from the authorities. There was a time when even all phone calls were eavesdropped on. The North Korean regime, which did not want the children announcing their hardships to the outside world, began censoring the children's letters. And by the end of 1962, the letters were completely cut off. In the end, the children experienced the pain of losing parents twice."
> — Sylwia Szyc, Polish researcher of North Korea

They all felt the pain of parting. Some children even suffered from homesickness. The children experienced frustration and loss as their only consolation, writing letters, was cut off. The children returned

North Korean war orphans at Kim Il Sung Academy in Valeč, Czechoslovakia, circa 1955.

to North Korea and tried their best to keep in contact with their European friends and teachers. But it was not easy for them to send the letters.

It was the letters that the Eastern European friends and teachers we met most treasured. The letters were the only thing left that connected them with the children. Perhaps the children who returned to North Korea were also waiting for a reply from their teachers and friends for a long time. Unfortunately, there was no way to know what became of the children who returned to North Korea after the correspondence was stopped. With heavy hearts, we headed to Poland, for the next leg of our journey.

CHILDREN FROM NORTH KOREA 67

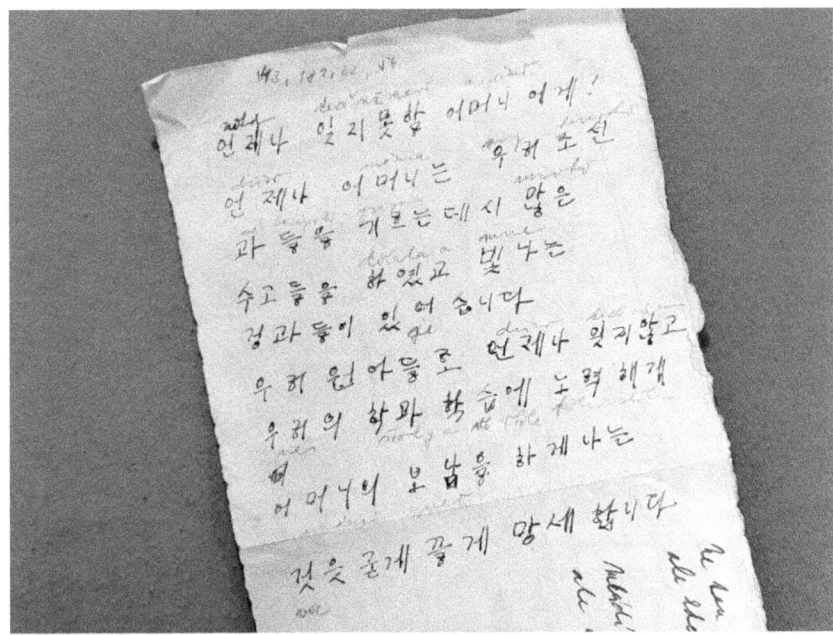

A letter from a North Korean child, found in the Czech Republic, that begins: "To my mother, whom I will never forget" (above). The many misspellings in the Korean text suggest that by that time, the children were more accustomed to Czech than Korean. The photo below is letters from North Korean children kept for 60 years by Polish teachers living in Pękowice, Poland.

CHAPTER 2

LANGUAGE DOESN'T MATTER WHEN YOU MEET GOOD PEOPLE

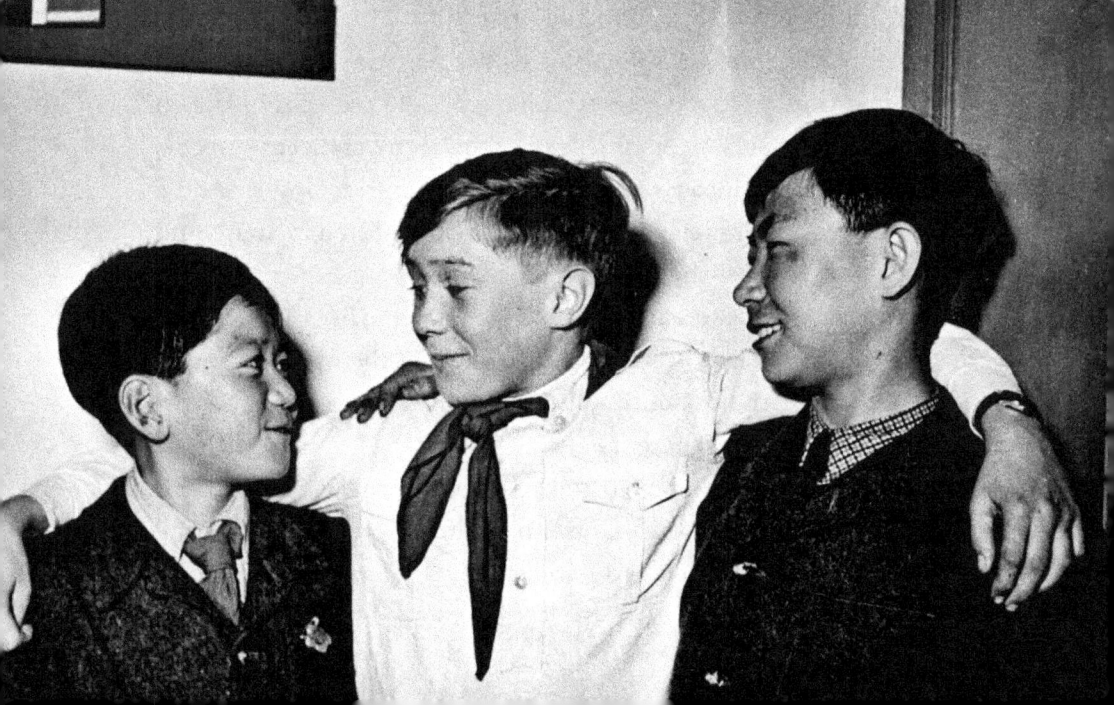

SOUTH AND NORTH KOREA DEALT WITH WAR ORPHANS IN DIFFERENT WAYS

It all started with the Korean War. On June 25, 1950, the Korean War was triggered when North Korean forces launched a surprise invasion of the South. This was the first military conflict of the Cold War. More than 1.14 million United Nations troops, including Republic of Korea (South Korea) and U.S. troops, were killed, injured, or missing. Losses on the communist side were also considerable, with 1.23 million troops from the Democratic People's Republic of Korea (North Korea) and China killed or missing. Civilian casualties totaled 3.58 million people in South and North Korea.

The forces of South and North Korea, representing capitalism and communism, respectively, clashed all over the Korean peninsula, in mountains and fields, rivers and seas. At the 38th parallel of latitude, Korea was divided into two states with different ideologies. And a new and unfamiliar life awaited the 100,000 children in South and North Korea who lost their parents in the war.

Wars always cause great damage to property and lives. Particularly devastating was the effect on children who lost their parents in the war. Neither North nor South Korea could offer proper facilities for children who lost their parents.

At this time, South and North Korea dealt with war orphans in different ways. South Korea chose to facilitate overseas adoption, while North Korea chose to outsource the orphans' education in

Greek war orphans who were sent to Poland to escape civil war, 1948.

Eastern Europe.

Neither South nor North Korea was able to take care of its war orphans by itself. Inevitably, they had to seek outside help.

In the case of North Korea, the Soviet Union, then the leader of the socialist world, played an indispensable role in making it possible for war orphans to collectively migrate to Eastern Europe and receive care and education. It was not a decision made by North Korea alone.

> "There were two important motives for sending North Korean orphans to Eastern Europe. The first was to strengthen solidarity between communist countries. The second was to acquire advanced technological skills. There were many coal mines in North Korea, but until then, coal mining techniques were learned from the Soviet Union. The idea was that sending children to Eastern Europe to learn skills there would help free North Korea's economic development from dependence on the Soviet

Union."

— Sylwia Szyc, Polish researcher of North Korea

The Korean War was not the first time in which left-wing governments sent war orphans abroad to receive a communist education. Previous examples include orphans from the Spanish Civil War being sent to the Soviet Union in 1937–1938. Hundreds of thousands of refugees were also displaced during the civil war in Greece between government forces and communist guerrillas from 1946 to 1949. They had to leave Greece and move to Eastern Europe. Long before the North Korean war orphans were sent to Eastern Europe, the Soviet Union had experience in accepting children from war-torn areas in other countries under the banner of fraternal socialism.

On March 4, 1948, Radio Free Greece, a mouthpiece of the Greek Communist Party, announced that children under the age of 15 would be moved to shelters set up by the Greece's provisional government. Numerous orphans who had lost their parents during the three-year war were already dying from malnutrition and infectious diseases.

The Greek Communist Party began to seek aid from the Soviet Union and its socialist allies in Eastern Europe. Its first measure in 1948 was the evacuation of 8,000 orphans from Greece to the Eastern bloc.

"After World War II, Serbian orphans came to Bulgaria, followed by North Korean children. Then they came from Vietnam, as well as from Afghanistan."

— Veselin Kolev, Bulgarian classmate

Bulgarian historian Jordan Baev.

Number of Greek war orphans accepted by Eastern European countries:
Romania 5,132
Czechoslovakia 4,148
Poland 3,590
Hungary 2,859
Bulgaria 672

"They went to Romania, Poland, Czechoslovakia, Hungary, and the Soviet Union. Some 62,000 to 70,000 Greek political immigrants migrated to Tashkent in Central Asia, which was then part of the Soviet Union. They were able to return to Greece after 30 years of military dictatorship. What this means is that, before the North Korean children came, Bulgaria had experience with taking care of them."

— Jordan Baev, Bulgarian historian

In Poland, the children from North Korea were sent to the village of Prochowice in the southwest (in the Śląski region). Prochowice was selected because there were many empty buildings there and it was relatively isolated. A mental hospital had been operating there since the 1940s; it was where mentally ill patients suffering war trauma were quarantined.

After World War II, kindergartens and dormitories for war orphans were established. In 1951, the first group of North Korean orphans arrived in Poland. Then, in 1953, a second group of over 1,000 orphans arrived.

At that time, Poland's Ministry of Foreign Affairs faced the considerable challenge of finding a place with suitable facilities, dorm rooms, and a hospital—a place that could house great numbers of children. It chose Prochowice.

Interestingly, Prochowice was already home to Greek and Macedonian children. Most of them were war orphans from the Greek Civil War or refugees who had fled Greece to escape the war. Eventually, the Greek children were moved to other areas so the North Korean children could be accommodated.

In the early 1950s, North Korean war orphans lived in Prochowice, Poland.

LEBENSBORN:
THE NAZI ETHNIC CLEANSING PLAN

Until 1945, Prochowice was German territory. The mental patients in Prochowice at the time were German. Under Nazi Germany, Prochowice had a dark history. It started with Heinrich Himmler, Hitler's closest confidant.

After the Nazis came to power, Hitler instituted a number of policies aimed at racial cleansing. One of them was the "Lebensborn" policy, a selective breeding experiment conducted in the name of protecting and strengthening the "Aryan race." It was a deeply racist plan that selected only the most "Aryan" individuals and nurtured them. And then the "T4 Project" was implemented. The T4 Project was a policy to isolate the disabled and mentally ill with the aim of strengthening the supposedly pure Aryan bloodline. Surprisingly, the place where these Nazi racial experiments were conducted was the very same place where the North Korean war orphans later stayed.

"The T4 Project was Hitler's racist policy. It was sort of a plan to get rid of people who were not needed by the Nazis. Its main targets were the disabled and the mentally ill. They tried to house them in one place and manage them. And according to the T4 Project plan, the mentally ill, the disabled, and later the Jews were

Lebensborn day care center operated as a result of the Nazis' selective breeding policy

forcibly mobilized and sacrificed for experiments. The Lebensborn project started with the aim of cultivating a superior Aryan race. Prochowice had a day-care center where children born to them were cared for."

—Sylwia Szyc, Polish researcher of North Korea

The plan to encourage "Aryan" parents belonging to the armed forces to have children was later spread throughout Germany and shifted toward selective breeding. Through Lebensborn, which means "the birth of life" or "the source of life," in 1939, 8,000 parents were subjected to selective breeding experiments.

Norwegian men were selected for the experiment based on the results of a study that found there were still many men in Norway considered to be of Aryan ancestry. In Germany and Poland, the victims were mostly women.

Even after the end of World War II, children born as a result of the Lebensborn policy were mostly illegitimate and abandoned. This was the tragic history of Prochowice.

THE 1950S: THE COLD WAR AND REGIME COMPETITION

The Western capitalist states coalesced into a collective security system through the North Atlantic Treaty Organization (NATO) in 1949. In response, the Soviet Union established the Warsaw Pact in 1955. Now the world was divided into two political and military blocs.

From competition in science and technology such as satellites to economic aid to developing Third World countries, the United States and the Soviet Union competed to try to prove their superiority.

Yuri Gagarin, who became the first person to orbit the Earth in 1961, and Valentina Tereshkova, who became the world's first female astronaut in 1963, became Soviet heroes, trying to show the world that the Soviet Union's level of science and technology surpassed that of the United States. They were heroes not just to the Soviet Union but to the whole socialist bloc.

The United States and the Soviet Union not only confronted each other but also competed to bring countries around the world into their respective camps. This is why the Soviet Union and the United States pursued a rivalry that led to space development, intercontinental ballistic missiles, and nuclear weapons. And ideological competition over human rights and humanitarian assistance was indispensable.

"What the Soviet Union was trying to achieve is clear. It intended to expand the communist bloc. It was already in Europe, in Asia, in Africa, and even in the Americas, right under the nose of the United States. If it became known that the Soviet Union was so devoted to helping the children of other countries, it would certainly help expand Soviet power."

— Jolanta Krysowata, Polish documentary director

The project to raise the North Korean war orphans in Eastern Europe was also planned in this context. The socialist camp, led by the Soviets, had to prove that it was superior to the capitalist states. In human rights and humanitarianism, it had to be ahead of the capitalist camp, including the United States. This was a time when the ideals and dreams of building a kind of socialist internationalism were ripening.

In the Eastern bloc, several literary works about the war orphans were written. In Poland, socialist reporter Marian Brandys visited the North Korean children at their dormitory, interviewed them, and then published a book about them called The House of Rediscovered Childhood. This book is of great value for its vivid depictions of the North Korean children's lives in Poland in the 1950s.

To raise the children from North Korea, Poland hired as many as 600 skilled workers. They included teachers and nannies, cooks, cleaners, nurses, and doctors.

The situation was similar in Romania. Interestingly, teachers and staff were required to sign confidentiality agreements, and the North Korean children were kept relatively isolated. At that time, few ordinary Europeans knew much about North Korea.

"All I knew about North Korea was that it was at war at the time. Around 1952, a map of Korea was hung up on a bulletin board in our local village. Light bulbs on the map lit up to show where the armies were and who was winning the battles. That was when I first became interested in North Korea. Before that, I knew nothing about it. After completing my teaching job, I was assigned to a school, and the person in charge asked me: 'Did you know that war orphans from North Korea came to Romania?' It was then that I first learned that North Korean children had come to Romania.

"Hearing that story, I felt compassion. In Romania, there were many children who lost their parents in the war."

— Georgeta Mircioiu, teacher at the Korea People's School in Romania

Interestingly, all the socialist countries in Eastern Europe at the time tried to keep the North Korean children isolated. In Poland, a showcase dormitory was set up in Świder, near Warsaw, while 200 children were quietly sent to Gołotczyzna.

Located in southwest Poland, Prochowice received the most children—about 1,400—and it was an isolated place. The situation was similar in Bulgaria, Romania, and Czechoslovakia.

When the Eastern European states hired local teachers to educate and care for the North Korean war orphans, they gave priority to those from poor peasant or rural families and those who lost their parents in World War II. The intention was to entrust the children to teachers who could empathize with their circumstances. The Eastern European states also wanted to instill in the teachers the ideals of socialism and socialist internationalism. The teachers chosen for this assignment were provided with free lodging and meals, as well as relatively high salaries. This suggests that the placement of North Korean war orphans in Eastern Europe was carried out based on a detailed plan.

TRANS-SIBERIAN SPECIAL TRAIN

The first train carrying North Korean war orphans departed in October 1951. From Pyongyang, the North Korean capital, through Moscow, the train to Sofia, the capital of Bulgaria, crossed Eurasia with hundreds of children. And at the end of that year, as the Korean War was raging, trains arrived one after another in Warsaw, Poland; Băile Tușnad, Romania; Sofia, Bulgaria; and Budapest, Hungary.

As the train arrived in puffs of white smoke, those people who had been waiting for the train for several hours on the platform got up and went back to their seats. The crowd that came out was larger than they could have imagined. Some were carrying bouquets of flowers. Some women prepared food and water for the children, who had come a long way.

Finally, as the train's smoke cleared, the children jumped out of the train one by one. They were all dressed the same, in matching cotton clothes, hats, and green rubber shoes. There were even children carrying backpacks on their backs.

As soon as they got off the train, they lined up and seated themselves on the platform. Their eyes expressed complex emotions: fear of this unfamiliar place, relief that they had escaped the battlefield, and the sadness of losing their parents. As they got off the train, European children with sparkling eyes cheered and waved. Slowly, the North Korean children moved into the welcoming crowd.

"We all went out to the nearest station from here to greet the children. The children waved through the window even when the train didn't stop. We waved our hands and shouted.
One by one, the children jumped out of the train. The children had been staying for a few days in the Soviet Union, so they were all pretty clean. Everyone was wearing the same clothes, as the Red Cross gave them uniforms."

— Katya Panalotova, Bulgarian classmate of North Korean war orphans

"Many children slept on the train floor. It must have been quite difficult.
(The train journey) took more than 10 days, and it took another few days to get from there to Siret. The train cars were not divided into compartments and only had chairs;

North Korean war orphans arriving in Bulgaria in 1952 and citizens welcoming them.

also, the chairs were hard wooden chairs. If there had been a lot of space, they could have stretched their legs comfortably, but that was not the case."

— Georgeta Mircioiu

The children had watched their hometown villages turn to ruins in the war and suffered the loss of their fathers and mothers. But none of them could have foreseen what kind of life awaited them.

"The children were in bad shape. They had been barely rescued from war and bombed-out homes. They drank any kind of water and had skin problems, and some children had no hair. Most of the children had parasites, and some had pneumonia and bad coughs.
"But the biggest problem was war trauma. At night, they were scared and had nightmares and were emotionally unstable.

As a teacher, all I could do at first was to hug and comfort the children, especially those who screamed at night from anxiety. Though we gave them food, they didn't eat it and later wanted to eat rice, so we cooked rice."
— Georgeta Mircioiu

"I took really good care of the children. I provided five meals a day.... At that time, I wore rubber shoes, but North Korean children also wore leather shoes. We were poor too, but we had a good time sharing bread and things."
— Katya Panalotova

"Their wish back then was to spread butter on bread and eat it."
— Maria Yamalieva

A Polish proverb says, "A guest in the house is a god in the house." Although they were poor, the children were warmly welcomed everywhere. Over time, they became more than just guests.

HIDDEN HISTORY

Until the 1960s, North Korea was in much better economic condition than South Korea. Although history cannot be based on speculation, if the 5,000 to 10,000 North Korean war orphans living in Eastern Europe had been recruited to aid in the economic development of North Korea, the history of the Korean peninsula today might well have been different. For North Korea's economic development and social system could have developed faster. This is evident from the fact that the educated class played a major role in South Korea's economic development.

It has been argued that individual North Korean war orphans played important roles in the later development of North Korean society. In fact, a few elite individuals who had gone through the war orphan program were posted back to Europe as diplomats or interpreters in foreign missions, such as trade offices. However, they were not ordinary North Korean war orphans. Most of them were children of high-ranking officials.

In the course of my research, I discovered that, along with actual war orphans, North Korea sent children of high-ranking officials disguised as orphans. Given North Korea's poor domestic conditions in the 1950s, this was like a study-abroad opportunity for the children of the North Korean political elite. This fact later became known to European teachers, causing considerable friction.

After being repatriated, most ordinary North Korean war orphans were scattered and lived as coal mine workers or quarry workers. They had few if any opportunities to apply the skills and culture they had learned in Europe to help develop North Korea.

Why? The most convincing reason is that the children's futures were sacrificed to maintain and strengthen Kim Il Sung's monolithic ideological system. The *Juche* (national self-reliance) *ideology* and the campaign to exclude foreign influence were two sides of the same coin. The *Juche ideology* was strengthened in North Korean society in the 1960s, at the same time as foreign culture and influence was rejected. It was at this time that the country began to be completely closed to the outside. All such policies were ultimately intended to strengthen Kim Il Sung's power.

In order to maintain his system, Kim had to prevent the inflow of foreign culture. In particular, he feared that the free thinking of Europe would spread to North Korea. Though Kim himself had sent the orphans to Eastern Europe, paradoxically, he worried about the influence they might have once they returned home.

> "When they returned to North Korea, the children were not allowed to remain together. A train carrying children stopped in unnamed rural villages in North Korea and dropped them off in small groups, only one or two people at a time.
> After returning to North Korea, the children, who had lived like a family in Prochowice, Poland, were never able to see each other again. There would have been no opportunity for them to use what they had learned in Europe."
> — Stanisław Wachal, Polish schoolteacher

North Korean war orphans who lived in Prochowice, Poland.

"If you read the letters the children sent to Europe after returning to North Korea, you can see how they lived at that time. A letter from one child states that he was assigned to a quarry and that winter is coming and he has no materials for heating, so he has to go to the mountains to find firewood.

Letters from other children assigned to the mines also contain accounts of seeking food or struggling in similar circumstances. It may be that none of the children were successful; almost all appear to have had a poor life (working) in mines or quarries."

— Haeseong Lee, professor of Korean language, University of Wrocław, Poland

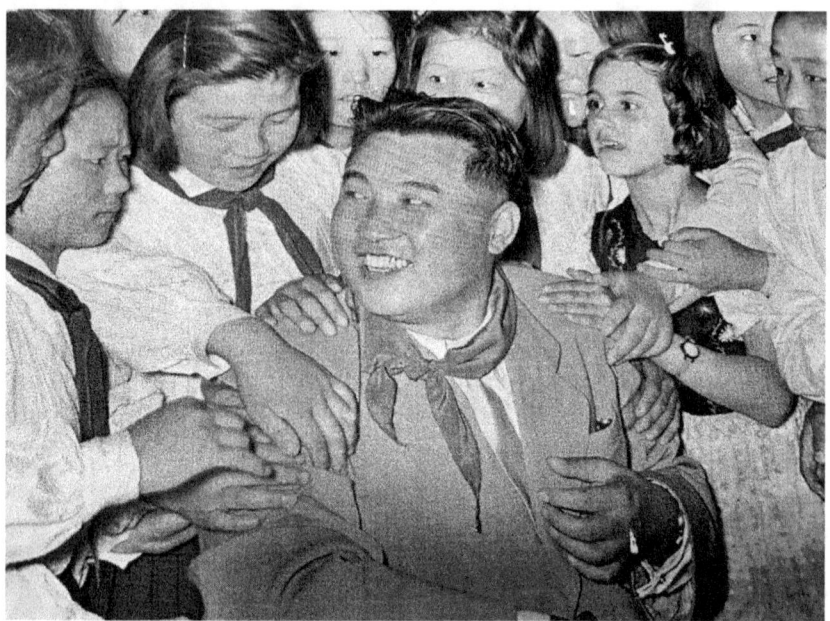
A picture of Kim Il Sung in Hungary, surrounded by North Korean war orphans.

North Korea's foreign policy since the 1960s can be summarized as anti-Soviet, anti-China, and self-reliant. The pretext was that North Korea was establishing its own independent policy. In reality, though, it was only a means to rationalize the system of Kim Il Sung's monolithic ideology. From Kim Il Sung's point of view, the North Korean war orphans in Eastern Europe, who had a more European way of thinking and a high level of education, were dangerous obstacles to the maintenance of his monolithic ideology system.

SMALL ARMY

What was the children's everyday life in Eastern Europe like? Newsreels were valuable materials through which to learn about the children's daily life. In particular, the newsreel on the Siret Korea People's School found in the National Film Archives in Romania revealed the daily activities of the children.

The lives of the North Korean children were governed by strict discipline. They all awoke at the same time and saluted the flag bearing Kim Il Sung's portrait. During the morning assembly, they had to start the day by singing "The Song of General Kim Il Sung." This morning assembly was held in all five Eastern European countries. This demonstrates how systematically the North Korean authorities tried to manage and control the children.

In a small group of about 10 people, there was a class leader, and there was a leader who monitored them. Their lives were thoroughly organized and managed. Individual freedom was not allowed. It was a life incongruous with the free atmosphere of Europe.

> "Groups of North Korean student leaders and North Korean students sometimes met each other as they crossed from the school building to the cafeteria. At that time, we taught them to be polite and to greet each other."
> — Georgeta Mircioiu

> "It seems that even among the teachers who came with (the North Korean war orphans), there was a minder among them. They thoroughly monitored and checked whether children were properly educated."
> —Haeseong Lee, professor of Korean language, University of Wrocław, Poland

In fact, the intense discipline and indoctrination of young children at the boarding school for North Korean war orphans was well documented. The newsreel found in Romania showed scenes of military parades and ceremonial training. I felt as if I were seeing soldiers marching through Kim Il Sung Square on the anniversary of North Korea's Foundation Day, which Pyongyang uses to promote itself to the outside world.

The children marched in formation, carrying flags that were too big for them. It must have taken considerable time and intensive drilling for them to be able to move their hands and feet in unison. Nevertheless, the children in the newsreel bore expressions of pride and determination.

Although they were receiving assistance from other socialist countries, the North Korean authorities took various measures to inspire national pride. Ideological education and military-style training were typical examples. Through training, the children were indoctrinated to value the group rather than the individual. And they were raised to be loyal not to the country but to one person, Kim Il Sung.

> "As they marched, they lined up like soldiers. It was like a small army."
> — Lilka Anatasova, Bulgarian classmate of the North Korean war orphans

A scene from a newsreel on a military parade of North Korean war orphans, found in Romanian archives. From the movie *Kim Il Sung's Children*.

"'Turn around!' 'Turn right!' 'Go forward!' I still remember these Korean phrases."

— Petrov Kolev, Bulgarian classmate of the North Korean war orphans

"The children had a lot of chores to do, such as tidying up the dormitory bedroom. The dorm floor was painted red, and the kids had to polish the floor. The kids had to go to school at 8 a.m., so I had to wake them up at 6:30. The room always had to be neat and tidy. Later, when the inspector came to school, if the room wasn't tidy, it was a big problem. There was a strict regimentation."

— Stanisław Wachal, Polish teacher

DEFEAT WAS DEATH

The North Korean children were segregated by gender. Not only in the dormitories but also in the classrooms, it was rare for boys and girls to be together. This patriarchal tradition continued in their new Eastern European context. For girls, the virtues of obedience and temperance were emphasized, while for boys, toughness was the highest value.

> "The girls from Korea were short. They were like our Polish girls. They were very clean and beautiful.
> The girls were very dexterous. They did a great job sewing. The children even presented embroidered handkerchiefs to Polish teachers."
> — Halina Dovek, Polish teacher

In general, there were more boys than girls. This was because North Korea preferred boys over girls when selecting and sending war orphans. Initially, the North Korean authorities intended to have the children learn advanced technical skills in Europe and then to place them in national reconstruction projects after they returned home. The idea was for the orphans to acquire construction, civil engineering, or coal mining know-how and apply it after returning to North Korea to help the country develop.

North Korean war orphans playing volleyball at the Korea People's School in Romania.

However, the girls demonstrated better bonding and communication skills. This was why the girls generally maintained closer relationships with their European friends than the boys did. From the point of view of European teachers and friends, it was much easier to communicate with calm and obedient girls than with the boys, who wanted only to be tough and strong.

> "The girls were very obedient and good listeners. I have a lot of good memories of them.
> The boys, on the other hand, were a little different. They were very disciplined. They were very well trained and strong."
> — Dovek, Polish teacher

While they were living in Eastern Europe, boys were given many classes to improve their physical strength. In particular, athletic competitions were a very important class and a kind of training. The children hated losing. Defeat was like death. The boys were particularly strong in soccer and volleyball. In any sports match, the

North Korean boys gave their all throughout the entire game. Though physically weaker, they played on an equal footing with the European children. They made up for their physical condition with their sheer determination. As a result, the North Korean children often won matches.

> "Polish children and North Korean children often had physical education classes together.
> When sports were played, the North Korean children often won, and our Polish boys were very disorganized.
> There were also some conflicts. Once there was a fight, and I was the mediator and I stopped it.
> To the North Korean children, I said, 'Listen, you guys, you are in our country and we love you. I don't want you guys to be angry or offended. Calm down.' We calmed the children down.
> I think the North Korean boys were stronger. Our Polish children always lost."
> —Halina Dovek

Why did North Korean boys play sports as if it was combat? This had to do in part with the trauma of war lingering in the children's psyche. Children who had lost everything in the war decided that they did not want to lose anything anymore.

Even in sports competitions where they could have laughed and enjoyed themselves, the children played fiercely out of a kind of survival instinct, to survive in an unfamiliar place.

FIERCE OFFSPRING

In Hungary, the North Korean children stayed on the outskirts of Budapest, in an area known as Hűvösvölgy, at the Pak Den Aj (Pak Chong-ae) Orphanage. In order to find this place, I had to ask local residents.

About 500 North Korean children are known to have stayed in Hungary. Most of them lived in or near Budapest. Hungary was the site of the first major anti-Soviet uprising in Eastern Europe: the 1956 Hungarian Revolution. Due to Western influence, the longing for freedom in Hungary was higher than elsewhere in Eastern Europe, and there was also a great deal of anti-Soviet sentiment.

When North Korean children arrived in the 1950s, the Hungarian Communist Party mandated that North Korean children should study side-by-side with Hungarian children. Unlike in Romania and Poland, which had large populations, in Hungary, hosting children in separate facilities was politically and financially burdensome. The Hungarian program encouraged North Korean children to adapt quickly by having them take classes with Hungarian children.

In the MTV Archives in Hungary, several photos showing the life of North Korean children in Hungary in the 1950s were found. The children in the photos were participating in art and cultural events. There were also classes on science and technology.

There were also indications that Hungary sought not to segregate but to integrate the North Korean children. Although it may have been for propaganda purposes, Hungary held more formal events and cultural education programs for the war orphans than any other country did. In the records we found many high-quality photos, taken by professional photographers. In the photos, North Korean and Hungarian children appeared to enjoy posing together, as if they were siblings. The atmosphere was evidently freer than in other Eastern European countries.

However, after the Hungarian Revolution of 1956, relations with North Korea gradually deteriorated. In fact, some North Korean students who were staying in Budapest at the time participated in the Hungarian Revolution. They were immediately caught by the North Korean embassy in Hungary and forcibly returned to North Korea. These measures show how closely North Korea was monitoring the liberalization movement then taking place in Eastern Europe. Many North Korean students went to study at the Budapest Institute of Technology, but in the 1960s, their number declined sharply.

Though it was difficult, I was able to find the children's former orphanage, located on the outskirts of Budapest. I arrived there and asked to film, but the institution did not readily allow it. The reason was that it is still operating as an orphanage—now for Hungarian children—and wanted to protect the children's privacy.

We could barely get permission to film outside the building, and then only in the space that the North Korean children had used. In the playground stood old, rusty parallel bars that the North Korean children might have played on 70 years ago. The parallel bars were so old that the wood was brittle and no one could stand on it any longer. Though the children were long gone, I half-expected their spirits to appear out of nowhere, running around and chatting. The children played and competed with European children on those parallel bars. Their European classmates remembered that many of the North Korean children had highly developed motor skills.

> "What was striking was that the children did not get tired easily."
> — Nikolov Voyajeev, Bulgarian classmate of North Korean war orphans

> "There was a game where we kicked a small object with feathers. We also competed to see who could kick it the longest without dropping it on the ground."
> — Petrov Kolev, Bulgarian classmate of North Korean war orphans

According to their Eastern European friends and teachers, the North Korean children were reluctant to admit defeat when playing sports. For the children, even winning or losing the game was a matter of survival. The idea that only the strong can survive trained the children to become stronger.

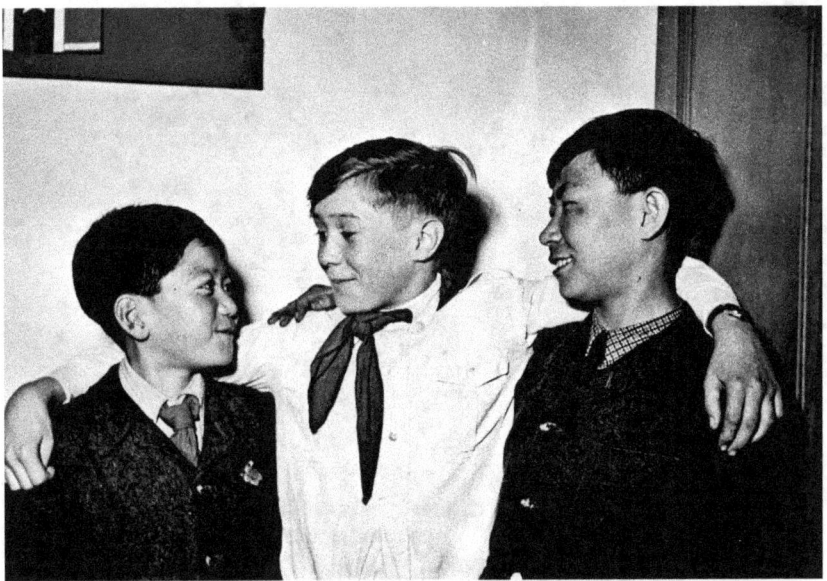

A North Korean war orphan and a Hungarian classmate.

A North Korean child in class with Hungarian students. Classes were held in Hungarian at the time.

"The North Korean children were hot-tempered and united. When there was a fight, unlike the Romanians, they fought until the other side lost. They were fierce. It was only after a full fight that they became as quiet as a mouse."

— Jean Pierre Thomas, janitor of the Korea People's School of Siret, Romania

WALK TO EUROPE

The children's schools, which were each called either "Korea People's School" or "Kim Il Sung Academy," were strictly controlled. The children awoke at 6:30 every morning, did group gymnastics, and then lined up. Then they raised their hands and saluted the flag bearing Kim Il Sung's portrait.

By the mid-1950s, a few of the war orphans in Eastern Europe had been sent back to North Korea. This included children suffering from mental illness, war trauma, and/or confusion over their national identity. These children were sent back in secret. The North Korean authorities must have been concerned that the children who remained in Eastern Europe would be psychologically shaken by their classmates' sudden repatriation.

However, it was not only the maladjusted children who were sent back to North Korea early. So-called "problem children" who made trouble at school or crept out of and back into the dormitory were also included. The story of one such child, named Won Dun-cheon, was particularly shocking.

Won Dun-cheon is remembered as a bright child. In fact, because he was so smart, he was nicknamed "Maxim," after the boy in the then-popular Soviet film Maximka (1953). In the film, Maxim is rescued by Russian sailors and grows up on a ship, becoming a smart and lively child.

Like the main character in the movie, Won Dun-cheon was also passionate about everything and solved problems creatively.

However, Dun-cheon did not like the North Korean style of education. It clashed with the relatively free atmosphere of Eastern European life. Thus, Dun-cheon broke the school rules and often climbed the fence to escape from school.

He was a curious child and wanted to see the wider world. He skipped class and asked questions that teachers couldn't answer. In the end, the North Korean authorities categorized Won Dun-cheon as one of the maladjusted children and sent him back to North Korea. That was the beginning of the tragedy.

Student Won Dun-cheon, who lived in Prochowice, Poland, was repatriated to North Korea. He set out on foot to return to Poland and died near the border between China and Korea.

> "(Won Dun-cheon) was about 12 years old. Even when he was in Poland, he messed up in class and ran away, and then he was treated as a problem child. The boy was said to have been very smart and kind.
> So initially, in 1956, about 20 children were returned to North Korea. Most of them were sick or depressed, and he was sent away with them.
> Later, the children who went to North Korea wrote letters to the Prochowice teachers. According to the letters, Won Dun-cheon drowned in a swamp while trying to cross the border to China and walk to Poland."
>
> — Haeseong Lee, professor of Korean language, University of Wrocław, Poland

The idea of walking all the way to Poland was surprising enough, but it was even more surprising that the 12-year-old had actually attempted it.

What made Won Dun-cheon try to walk back to Poland? Perhaps there was a connection between the North Korean war orphans and their friends and teachers from Eastern Europe that we cannot fully understand. Maybe he had an urgent reason to try to go back. Dun-cheon's death leaves many questions unanswered.

LANGUAGE DOESN'T MATTER WHEN YOU MEET GOOD PEOPLE

The North Korean children initially struggled to adjust due to differences in language and culture. However, as time passed, they adapted to their European surroundings. More and more of the children made friends with Europeans and got along well with their teachers. In this context, the consideration and dedication of the European teachers were indispensable.

> "I once asked a fellow teacher: 'How did you communicate in the classroom when you didn't understand the language?' He replied, 'We communicated well, without any problems.'
> I'm not sure what language they spoke in when they had a conversation. A wise man once said, 'Language doesn't matter when you meet good people.'"
> — Halina Dovek, Polish teacher of North Korean war orphans

Although the North Korean war orphan program started for ideological reasons in the context of the Cold War, at the ground level, it involved encounters between well-meaning human beings. European teachers tried to treat the children without any prejudice. The fact that most of the European teachers were very young also had a big impact on their encounter. In Poland, Romania, and

Bulgaria, teachers between the ages of 17 and 19 were assigned to Korea People's Schools. For most of them, it was their first teaching assignment.

> "The (European) teachers who came at this time were from poor peasant families, and in fact, many of them had lost their parents during World War II. 'Let us be mothers and fathers to children who have lost their parents. Let's heal the pain of those children.' It is said that many teachers had such a heart.
> There were many kinds of people at school, such as teachers who taught at the school, nannies who took care of the children and put them to sleep, and other types of people like cooks, cleaners, and laundry people. But that's why they told the kids to call them all Mom and Dad."
> — Sylwia Szyc, Polish researcher of North Korea

North Korean children were provided with an abundance of food, prepared by professional chefs, and the best living conditions possible at the time. Given Eastern Europe's postwar economic difficulties, it was a real extravagance.

> "When the children first came, it was very difficult because they couldn't get used to Polish food. But within a year, they got used to Polish food. After that, they even eagerly ate dishes like macaroni."
> — Stanisław Wachal, Polish teacher of North Korean war orphans

The recollections of Halina Dovek, a teacher who taught children in Otwock, near Warsaw, Poland, and Stanisław Wachal, a teacher in Prochowice, show that caring for the children at the time was not an easy task. It took heartfelt affection and consideration.

A group lunch at the Korea People's School in Romania.

Every aspect of these young children's lives had to be looked after, from eating, sleeping, and dressing to educating them. In addition, the orphans' war trauma needed to be dealt with.

However, most of the children from North Korea were unable to adapt to the unfamiliar European life. This maladaptation appeared both mentally and physically.

To keep these children healthy, the best doctors and nurses in the area were on call 24 hours a day. A newsreel discovered in Romania shows that a light aircraft was even stationed near the dormitory to transport patients in case a medical emergency arose.

Of the more than 5,000 North Korean children who lived in Eastern Europe, there were only four reported deaths there: two in Romania, one in Poland, and one in Bulgaria. The statistics might have been tampered with to lower the mortality rate, but in any case, the actual number must have been very small. This shows that Eastern European countries provided the best possible support for the children.

Near the Korea People's School in Siret, Romania, a light plane was on constant standby in case of a medical emergency. From the movie *Kim Il Sung's Children*.

Nevertheless, there were still many communication problems between the North Korean children and local teachers and medical staff. Especially in the children's first weeks in Eastern Europe, there were not many interpreters.

Izydor Urian, who served as Romanian ambassador to Pyongyang and Seoul, recounted an interesting anecdote in that regard.

> "Most of the children were not in good health.
> The children kept saying 'A-pa,' but I didn't know exactly what those words meant.
> In Romanian, 'A-pa' means 'water.' So I called over a person from North Korea and asked what this child wanted. The child kept saying 'A-pa,' so I asked if it meant asking for water. Then he told me that the child was ill. There were so many things we didn't know."
>
> — Urian, former Romanian ambassador to North Korea

FRIENDSHIP TO LOVE

In 1953, the Korean War, which had dragged on for three years, finally came to an end. The news that the war was over reached Eastern Europe, including the North Korean children and teachers. In the meantime, the psychological pressure they had felt due to the war slowly began to ease. And gradually, they started to adjust to new European values and lifestyles.

The children from North Korea quickly adapted to life in Europe. As they became accustomed to the local language, their biggest problem—communication—was also eased. As the language barrier broke down, they began to forge deep friendships with European children. And sometimes friendship turned into affection. A change occurred in the children, who were accustomed to strict regimentation. The same was true of the North Korean teachers who settled in Europe with the young children. However, dating or marrying a foreigner was illegal. Amid the Cold War and international espionage, the atmosphere of suspicion of foreigners grew stronger.

Naturally, there were not many people who risked dating foreigners. However, it is natural for men and women to be attracted to each other and to fall in love. This cannot be artificially prevented.

> "In some cases, North Korean and Romanian students were dating. Not only the students but also the teachers were in love. When they got married, I saw them off at the station.
> If a North Korean married a Romanian, they couldn't live together in Romania. That was the rule....
> They were separated or repatriated to North Korea, with their children...."
>
> — Jean Pierre Thomas, janitor of the Korean People's School of Siret, Romania

The taboo on international dating and marriage was applied by North Korea and Eastern European countries alike. However, despite strict bans on dating by the local Communist Party, education authorities and North Korean officials, couples secretly fell in love everywhere.

Women such as Renata Hong from East Germany, Halina Ogarek-Czoj from Poland, and Georgeta Mircioiu from Romania married North Korean husbands and started families in Pyongyang during this period. They dated secretly and then formally applied for marriage approval.

In Romania, marriage to a foreigner had to be approved by the Central Committee. Georgeta Mircioiu was the first to have a marriage recognized by both the North Korean and the Romanian government. After getting married, Mircioiu and Cho Chung Ho secured visas from the North Korean embassy and moved to North Korea. They also had a child. However, their happy life together did not last long.

As the liberalization wave in Europe and the campaign to exclude foreigners in North Korea overlapped, couples like them were forced to separate. There were even cases of forced divorce. This phenomenon continued until the early 1960s.

> "The North Korean side did not recognize marriage to a foreign national, even a citizen of another communist country. In particular, it was considered illegal to marry a foreign woman.
> Foreigners who married North Koreans were forced to leave North Korea with their children. So 1962 could be said to be the first year of the isolation of North Korea as we know it today."
> — Sylwia Szyc, Polish researcher of North Korea

Between 1953 and 1956, people could date freely. However, in 1956, the situation changed drastically. Personal contacts or meetings became more difficult. This was because North Korea had chosen the path of isolation and closure.

In Prochowice, Poland, there was a secret love affair between a North Korean man named Jun and a Polish woman named Krysia. Likewise, there was a secret relationship between a female North Korean teacher, Ri Su-ok, and a Polish man named Marek. In both cases, the couples were forced to separate after their North Korean supervisors learned of their relationships. And in both cases, the North Korean partners were forcibly repatriated by North Korean agents. No one outside North Korea has been able to determine their whereabouts since.

> "It all happened around the same time. In Poland, Romania, East Germany, and so on, some foreign students from North Korea started families with locals. They were all forced to divorce.
> Strictly speaking, they were divorced.
> Halina Ogarek-Czoj, who taught the Korean language at the University of Warsaw, was eventually forced to divorce and was deported despite living in Pyongyang for a while after giving birth to a daughter.

> Then, in 1986, there was an official visit to North Korea by the Polish leader, Wojciech Jaruzelski.
> During the summit, Ogarek-Czoj, a grandmother, begged, 'Please let me meet my husband just once,' but she was not allowed to meet him, even though she was an interpreter for the summit at that time."
>
> — Haeseong Lee, professor of Korean language, University of Wrocław, Poland

The forced separation and divorce measures between North Koreans and Eastern Europeans were connected to the exclusion campaign that began in North Korea in 1959. The North Korean state separated loving couples in a variety of ways, including through psychological pressure by forcibly relocating one of them to a place where there were no outsiders, and through economic pressure such as reducing stipends for groceries or ending rent subsidies. However, because some couples still did not separate, the regime made international marriages illegal and forced them to divorce. These racist and xenophobic policies were completely unjustified.

A Polish woman who wished to remain anonymous lived in Pyongyang until 1962, when she was deported from North Korea. She entered the Polish embassy in Pyongyang to protest the Polish Communist Party's refusal to take any diplomatic action against North Korea's interference with international marriages. However, the North Korean authorities did not respond.

Eventually, she fell into despair and attempted suicide. Fortunately, she survived and returned to Poland with the couple's son and moved to a rural village. There, she met a Polish man and lived the rest of her life, yet died heartbroken.

The key to understanding North Korea's closed society lies in such attempts to control even the natural emotions of humans. Individuals' freedom, values, and pursuit of happiness have always been pushed to the background due to policies that prioritize the

Krysia and Jun, who had fallen in love in Poland, were forced to separate.

Marek (second from left in the front row) and Ri Su-ok (far right in the back row), a couple. As news of their relationship became known, Ri Su-ok, a teacher, was suddenly repatriated to North Korea, and they never met again.

collective and the monolithic ideological system centered on Kim Il Sung. More and more people became resentful of a system in which they had to get the party's permission even to date, and they had to report on their private lives.

But why did the North Korean authorities ban loving relationships that crossed borders and races? In fact, as a result of such measures, foreign nationals living in Pyongyang who married

North Koreans were deported until the early 1960s.

Why did they force even married couples to separate for life? Numerous questions arose. There was only one solution: I had to speak firsthand to people who had married North Koreans.

We headed to Bucharest, the Romanian capital, in search of a woman who had been waiting 60 years to reunite with her North Korean husband. Her husband was Cho Chung Ho. He was the same man who, in 1951, accompanied about 3,000 North Korean war orphans to Siret, Romania. In the story of Mircioiu and Cho Chung Ho, the sadness and pain of modern Korean history lurked everywhere.

CHAPTER 3

CANDLES FOR THE LIVING

GEORGETA MIRCIOIU: A WOMAN WAITING FOR HER NORTH KOREAN HUSBAND

"It is said that a Polish teacher asked a North Korean in the 1950s, when North Koreans and Poles were living together in Prochowice: 'Why can't you guys marry our Polish girls?' The man replied, 'We can only do what the party allows us to do. The party has never allowed us to love a foreign woman.'"

— Krysowata, Polish documentary director

Jolanta Krysowata, who made a 2006 documentary about North Korean war orphans in Poland, interviewed a Polish woman who fell in love with a North Korean man at that time, married him, and gave birth to a child. According to the woman's testimony, dating a North Korean man was considered unnatural and dangerous. Above all, there was no guarantee that he would be able to stay in Europe if they married. All the North Korean students and teachers could potentially be called back to North Korea at any time. In order for the family to remain together, European women had to go to their husband's homeland: North Korea.

Conflicts began in the late 1950s, when North Korea adopted its anti-Soviet, anti-Chinese isolationist policy. Thereafter, a campaign took place in North Korea to unconditionally reject foreigners,

Romanian woman Georgeta Mircioiu and North Korean teacher Cho Chung Ho, a couple.

foreign cultures, and foreign ideas. This was when Kim Il Sung locked all the outside doors to his kingdom.

But heartfelt love between people could not be stopped. Even under these unfavorable conditions, a few Europeans dated or lived with North Koreans. Their love transcended all obstacles, including economic disadvantages and personal threats.

The North Korean men they loved came from a war-torn land of poverty and despair. That was why people around them discouraged such relationships. Falling in love with a man who never knew when he might have to return to the North was risky. However, the women braved these obstacles one by one.

Not many people can easily give up on a love that started with such obstacles. Even after being forced to part with their North Korean husbands, European women waited eagerly to reunite with them. Each had her own story.

"I remember a Polish woman waiting for her North Korean husband. She said the two had a difficult marriage, and they had a child together. The child was given his father's surname, Yun. The child had never seen his father's face.
I met the woman, and she said to me, 'It's hot in summer, so I sleep with the door open. When I sleep with the door open, I hear a noise outside, and whenever I hear footsteps, I turn around to see if it is him.' Even now, when I think of her, my heart aches."

— Jolanta Krysowata, Polish documentary director

A similar situation occurred to a Romanian woman around the same time. Her name is Georgeta Mircioiu; she was born in 1934. She also married a North Korean man and has a daughter. She had to part from her husband in Pyongyang in 1962 and is still desperately searching for him 60 years later. The man she is looking for is named Cho Chung Ho.

KOREAN DICTIONARY WITH 160,000 WORDS

Mircioiu currently lives in Romania's capital, Bucharest, with her daughter, son-in-law, and granddaughter. Although many years have passed, she still cannot forget her love for her husband, Cho Chung Ho. She hasn't ever moved from the house she lives in, just in case her husband comes back.

She lived her whole life without losing hope that one day, she would be able to see her husband again. To hold on to her memories of him, she started studying Korean. She studied Korean on her own, an intensive effort that recently came to fruition when she published two dictionaries. Her Korean-Romanian dictionary contains 130,000 words, and her Romanian-Korean dictionary contains 30,000 words. Combined, the two dictionaries have over 160,000 words.

She entered all those words into her notebook in longhand. She devoted several decades to completing the two dictionaries. Why did she work on them for so long?

"It was possible because I did not lose hope that my husband would come back. I worried that, if my husband returned after so many years, we would not be able to communicate with each other. Because he would have forgotten all the Romanian words.

Mircioiu holding her two dictionaries, containing a total of 160,000 words.

> At that time, I started working on a dictionary, thinking that it might be possible to have a conversation using the dictionary."
> — Georgeta Mircioiu, a Romanian woman waiting for her North Korean husband

People tend to try to put old, unnecessary or bad memories behind them. But for Mircioiu, forgetting would mean a final goodbye to her husband. She could not give up the belief that her husband would come back alive. In Georgeta Mircioiu's dictionary, her own sadness and dedication intersect.

In February 2019, I visited Mircioiu's home in Bucharest again after 15 years. Since the first time I met her at her apartment in 2004, nothing had changed. It was an apartment in an apartment house built during communism. In her residential area on Mosilor Street, the buildings were neatly lined up in a row, like matchboxes.

Although many years have passed, Mosilor Street has not changed at all—from the flower shop across the street to the restaurant next to the apartment entrance. In Europe, it can sometimes feel as if time has stopped. Europeans sometimes seem to be immune to change and to keep things that are old and outdated. Everywhere on the street, I could feel an atmosphere similar to that of Mircioiu waiting for her husband.

I stopped by a flower shop to buy a bunch of roses. I suddenly remembered buying a bouquet of flowers there 15 years earlier, when I first visited. The flower shop owner was the same person.

The florist made a pretty bouquet by mixing red roses and white mistletoe. Perhaps because it was early in the morning, the refreshing scent of roses tickled the tip of my nose.

After I rang the doorbell and waited for about five minutes in the apartment building's lobby, Mircioiu took the elevator down to the front door. Aside from her now-white hair, nothing about Mircioiu had changed. I presented her with the flowers. Seeing how happy she was holding them, I suddenly imagined what she must have been like when she was 19 and first met the man who would become her husband. She was a courageous woman who fell in love with a North Korean man without hesitation, and a trusting woman who has been waiting for 60 years to reunite with her husband. Just meeting her again was a heartbreaking event.

After a while, she led me into the living room. The furniture and cabinets and the paintings on the walls were the same as before. There was a framed picture of her daughter wearing a traditional Korean outfit, a *hanbok* (known as *saekdong jeogori*), which she said had been brought from North Korea. Everything felt familiar. To my surprise, nothing had changed in 15 years. This was evidence that she didn't want to change. She did not give up hope that she would be reunited with her husband.

Moments later, she entered the living room with a tray full of tea and cookies. As soon as she sat down, the first thing she brought out was her dictionaries. She had every reason to be proud of them.

Imagine how hard it must have been for an ordinary individual to translate 160,000 words for dictionaries. When I first met her in 2004, she was still preparing the dictionaries. I remembered her paper drafts piled up on the table next to the desk.

The manuscripts she was working on at that time were published as two dictionaries. As I captured her image on camera, I was impressed. I took the dictionary she handed me and turned the pages. It was the size of a large encyclopedia volume and weighed quite a bit. As I touched the thick volume, I could feel her tenacity. It took her over 30 years to publish it—the work of a lifetime.

It was an honorable task and a challenge for anyone. Relying on a pair of high-power magnifying glasses, she translated Romanian words into Korean until her hair turned white. She said that each time she wrote down a word, she thought of her husband.

As she wrote down the word "love," the moments she and her husband shared together flashed past. As she wrote, her hopes rose that her husband would be able to return to his family. Whenever she felt like giving up, she resolved instead to write down more Korean words. Thus, the words in her dictionary represented a story written with sadness and tears. Why did she still keep her husband, Cho Chung Ho, in her heart?

DRAMATIC LIFE JOURNEY

The stories that Mircioiu told me in 2004 were shocking. From the migration of nearly 3,000 children from North Korea to Romania, to her secret international four-year relationship, her approved marriage and relocation to Pyongyang, and the process of being deported from North Korea and living apart from her husband—it was like a drama.

Her stories were a hidden history that was not known in South Korea until then. In the life of this ordinary woman, through the Cold War, the ideological confrontation over the Korean peninsula, the North Korean campaign to exclude foreigners, and the establishment of the *Juche ideology*, the whirlwind of history unfolded.

However, to confirm her account, we needed more information about the North Korean war orphans living in Eastern Europe in the 1950s. While I captured her daily life on camera, I hired local residents to find documentation on the North Korean war orphans. For this work, I recruited a Korean student who was then attending the University of Romania.

It was not easy to find data from 60 years ago. At that time, old materials had not yet been catalogued digitally, so they had to be searched for by hand.

I visited the National Film Archives in Romania, the National Library of Romania, and the University of Bucharest library and

North Korean war orphans arriving in Romania in 1951.

searched through the old materials one by one.

Near the end of my 10-day tour in Romania, I received a call from a Korean student saying that he had found the material. Checking the data was not easy. Even now, those moments are vivid in my memory. For the first time, we could see with our own eyes the actions of North Korean war orphans in Eastern Europe.

After the Korean War broke out in 1950, Romanian Communist Party newspapers began to report on Korea. We found an article about North Korean children arriving in Romania in 1951.

At the National Film Archives in Romania, we also learned there was a four-and-a-half minute 35mm newsreel showing the daily life of North Korean children.

The next day, we arrived at the National Film Archives with Mircioiu and watched the 1953 newsreel. As the film was being shown, Mircioiu seemed to travel back in time to Siret, where she had lived with these children. Whenever a familiar face appeared on the screen, she called out the child's name.

In Siret, Romania, outdoor classes were occasionally held. Choi Soon-ok, a North Korean who taught Korean language classes for children under the age of five. From the movie *Kim Il Sung's Children*.

Do you remember the names of those children?

"Of course. The child blowing the trumpet was named Park Min-do. The name of the teacher who was teaching North Korean children was Choi Soon-ok. She used to teach Korean classes under a tree.

The child I remember the best was named Shin Tae-geun. He was always smiling brightly. He came to Romania with his younger sibling. He would always run to me and hold me in his arms. He was so cute. He was very smart and friendly. I once heard that he was working for the North Korean embassy in France. But we never met again. I really miss him."

Mircioiu's 2004 testimony that North Korean teacher Choi Soon-ok taught Korean under a tree was proven to be true through a newsreel we discovered in Romania in 2019. The footage shows children as young as five years old studying Korean under a tree.

"I don't know how many years it's been since I saw the children. I wonder how everyone is doing. All the children were kind and sincere."

Mircioiu suddenly pointed a finger at a girl's face as she appeared on the screen. "That child is Jeong Suk-ja. She was the kid who followed me the most." The sight of the girl moved her to tears. Sixty years later, she remembered the children's names correctly.

As I took a picture of her, I couldn't say anything. That was the moment when the history of North Korean children, buried and forgotten over time, was revealed. The memories of that day in 2004 are still vivid in my mind.

According to Mircioiu, a total of 3,000 North Korean children came to Romania—the most of any of the five countries in Eastern Europe that accepted them. The children were later dispersed among various cities in Romania. The vast majority of them, 2,700, went to Siret; among them, 500 children from grades one to four and about

Mircioiu standing with North Korean children at the Korea People's School in Siret, Romania. The second girl from the left was Jeong Suk-ja, who followed Mircioiu the most.

700 from grades five to eight were moved to Târgoviște, near Bucharest.

Not only war orphans but also high school and college students with parents were included. And secretly, North Korea also sent selected children of the elite to live with the war orphans so they could benefit from study abroad.

CHO CHUNG HO: A NORTH KOREAN MAN

To educate and supervise the war orphans, the North Korean authorities dispatched a dozen North Korean teachers along with the children. In Siret, Romania, a boarding school for the orphans, called the Korea People's School, was established. The school's principal was Cho Chung Ho.

Meanwhile, Mircioiu, a 19-year-old who had just graduated from teaching school, was given a job as an art teacher. Although she didn't even know exactly where Korea was on the world map, Mircioiu took care of the orphaned children as if they were her own.

In the spring of 1953, as the North Korean children gradually began to adjust to life in Romania, a turning point came in Mircioiu's life. It started with a small flower basket symbolizing the Romanian custom called Mărțișor.

> "On the day to celebrate spring, Romanian teachers got together and made Mărțișor ornaments until late at night. I made dolls for boys and girls and made flower baskets by twisting silk threads.
> I was tired that day, so I went to bed early, but the other teachers stayed up all night to make them.
> The next morning, the other teachers were tired and couldn't get up. A fellow Romanian teacher said,

'Mircioiu, you didn't make the gifts and went to bed early, so you bring the things we made to the North Korean teachers.' So I went to the male North Korean teachers and gave them out. Everyone liked them."

— Georgeta Mircioiu

The Mărțișor celebration, which comes in spring, was also an opportunity for young Romanians to confess their love to someone. At that time, male teachers from North Korea were intriguing to Romanian women, because most of them were good-looking and had a good physique. Perhaps the North Korean authorities placed great importance on appearance when selecting teachers to send to Eastern Europe.

"I went to Principal Cho with the last remaining Mărțișor ornament. When I delivered the gift, his first question was 'Who made this?' I didn't know who made it, so I just named a female teacher I was close to. Suddenly he said, 'I won't accept it,' with a serious face.
I was embarrassed, and when I was about to open the door and go outside, he said, 'Wait a minute. Let's talk.'
At that time, the principal's office had a large map on the wall. It was painted in red with the borders of Europe and Asia. Looking at the map, Mr. Cho asked, 'Can you see the borders there?' I said yes. Then, suddenly, Mr. Cho said to me, 'There are borders on the map, but our friendship has no borders.'"

— Georgeta Mircioiu

Cho Chung Ho's statement, "Our friendship has no borders," moved Mircioiu's heart.

Cho Chung Ho, the principal of the Korea People's School, who accompanied 3,000 North Korean war orphans to Romania.

"A week after Mărțișor when we met and talked, a dance class was held for teachers to learn the waltz and the tango. Men and women were waiting for their turn to dance in pairs.
Until then, I practiced the steps alone, but during that week, I had time to dance in pairs. On that day, Principal Cho Chung Ho reached out his hand so that we could dance a waltz together. I was clumsy and stepped on his feet, but for me it was a pleasant and poignant moment."
— Georgeta Mircioiu

Over time, Mircioiu became attracted to Cho Chung Ho. Cho developed the same feelings. Mircioiu saw Cho as a sincere and responsible man who was always kind and caring to others.

"He always asked for my opinion.
'What are your thoughts?' 'What do you think?'
I really respected Cho Chung Ho. I feel so bad that this happened...."
— Georgeta Mircioiu

Cho Chung Ho served as the principal of the school for North Korean war orphans and a supervisor of the teachers. He was a responsible and diligent figure who shouldered the school's administrative tasks. He even built a swimming pool for the children and planted a vegetable garden to make them kimchi.

Whatever the situation, he tried to do his best for the children. He was a sincere person who took the lead rather than waiting for others to do so. As a result, he was respected not only by the North Korean teachers but also by the Romanian teachers and staff.

SECRET LOVE

On July 27, 1953, the Korean War, which had dragged on for three years, ended. The news that the Korean War was over was a great relief to North Korean children and teachers alike. From this period, romances began to occur between Europeans and North Koreans. At that time, dating or marriage with a foreigner was banned.

> "In the 1950s, Polish women faced many difficulties if they wanted to marry American, West German, or British citizens. The Polish government would not even issue them a passport.
> They were not even allowed to leave the country. Naturally, many problems followed. But at least in the 1950s, if a Polish woman wanted to marry a citizen of another communist country, such as Czechoslovakia or East Germany, it wasn't a big deal. It can be said that the situation in Poland was much better than in North Korea."
>
> — Jolanta Krysowata, Polish documentary director

Georgeta Mircioiu, a Romanian teacher, and Cho Chung Ho, a North Korean principal, were dating, 1955.

The same was true of Mircioiu and Cho Chung Ho. The two started a secret relationship and, nearly four years later, began applying to the authorities of North Korea and Romania for official permission to marry.

> "One day, Mr. Cho gave me a dictionary. It was a Korean-Russian dictionary. He was going to give me a letter that I could translate and show to my parents that would ask them for permission to marry me. Inwardly, I wondered, 'Can I get married now even though the situation is difficult?' At that time, I had to get permission from the Central Committee to get married. But I couldn't say such a thing; I just said, 'I got it' and returned home with the letter Mr. Cho gave me."
>
> — Georgeta Mircioiu

The letter Cho gave, asking permission from Mircioiu's parents to marry him, was written in Russian because Cho did not speak Romanian well. In fact, because Mircioiu knew Russian, conversations between the two were mainly in Russian. Mircioiu then began translating Cho's letter into Romanian. Her mother happened to see her at that time. Her mother came to Mircioiu and carefully broached the subject of her relationship.

> "My mother said, 'Have you ever had a North Korean boyfriend?' Then she said, 'You can't have a North Korean boyfriend.' I couldn't even mention marriage at all.
> My mother went on to say, 'If someone you are involved with leaves for North Korea, you will be alone, and obviously you will be hurt.' She was trying to nip this in the bud.
> So, although I translated the letter, I returned to the school in Siret without even bringing up the marriage plan or giving the letter to my parents."
> — Georgeta Mircioiu

However, Cho Chung Ho was the kind of person who never gave up. And Mircioiu was the same. In 1954, Mircioiu applied to the Central Committee for permission to marry Cho. And Cho submitted documents to the North Korean authorities asking for their consent. Getting such permission was difficult, even if both the man and the woman involved were from communist countries.

In the spring of 1954, Cho Chung Ho came down with severe pneumonia. He was transferred from Siret to a general hospital in Bucharest, where he was tested and treated for six months. In January 1957, the North Korean embassy held a banquet to celebrate the new year. Cho and Mircioiu were also invited.

> "There, an embassy official announced he had good news from the Democratic People's Republic of Korea.
> It was the news that our marriage application had been officially accepted in both countries. I couldn't believe I was finally going to be the wife of a North Korean man."
> — Georgeta Mircioiu

Everyone has a special time in their life. Looking back, Mircioiu remembers the most beautiful time in her life as the time she was with Cho Chung Ho. Theirs was the first international marriage jointly recognized by Romania and North Korea. Sadly, however, their honeymoon did not last long. The North Korean authorities contacted the embassies of each country concerned, ordering all North Korean war orphans and students in Eastern Europe to return home.

Even for Mircioiu, who had entered newlywed bliss in Romania, change was inevitable. Mircioiu wanted to live with her husband in Romania. However, North Korea, her husband's home country, did not allow its citizens to freely decide their own destiny. The order to repatriate North Korean war orphans also applied to her husband. And if her husband returned to North Korea, she felt she had to go with him.

LIVING IN PYONGYANG AS A FOREIGNER

February 2019 was still cold. The winter snow had not yet melted, so the road was icy. Mircioiu, who was in her 80s, was preparing to go out. She was headed for the North Korean embassy in Romania. Sixty-five years earlier, she had gone there to submit a registration certificate to get married to Cho Chung Ho. And in 1959, she and her husband had gone there and held hands while they awaited their visa to enter North Korea.

Her husband is no longer with her to hold her hand, but she is still knocking on the North Korean embassy's door. She continues to make appeals to learn whether her husband is alive or dead. After being forced to leave Pyongyang in 1962, when she heard the news of her husband's disappearance, she took her young daughter in her arms and ran to this place. Years had passed, but the North Korean flag still fluttered in front of the embassy building.

Mircioiu remembers April 20, 1957, as the happiest and most meaningful day in her life. It was the day that she and Cho got married with permission from their respective governments. And two years later, in September 1959, the two first set foot in Pyongyang as a couple.

There were many difficult times before she met Cho for the first time in 1952, and the love they had nurtured for seven years came to fruition as they started their newlywed life in Pyongyang. As long as

A commemorative photo Georgeta Mircioiu took with her husband Cho Chung Ho's relatives in 1959, when she was just beginning her life in Pyongyang.

she was with her husband, she was sure she would be happy anywhere. Mircioiu remembered the moment she arrived:

> "When we arrived in Pyongyang, all of Cho Chung Ho's uncle's family came to meet us. He kissed my hand, like he knew he was supposed to kiss the back of a Romanian woman's hand when meeting her. I was so surprised then. I never thought that a North Korean would kiss my hand. I think it was some kind of respect for me. That moment was truly touching.
> The apartment we lived in was run by the People's Committee and was used by senior staff. It was near Moranbong Park, not far from the Taedong River, and his uncle's family lived there."
>
> — Georgeta Mircioiu

As soon as he arrived in North Korea, Cho was given a lot of work. He became a high-ranking official in the Ministry of Education. It seemed that the party highly valued him for safely leading the 3,000 North Korean war orphans in Romania back home. Mircioiu entered university and began studying Korean and French. It was a strange but happy life.

Cho, though busy, devoted a lot of time to Mircioiu. They lived their idyllic newlywed life, taking walks together along the Taedong River.

> "My house was close to Pyongyang Train Station, so I lived on the first floor of an apartment building that had an engineering institute, an opera house, and a hotel for foreigners. When I think about it, I was provided with fairly decent accommodations compared to the standard of living of North Koreans at the time."
> — Georgeta Mircioiu

TIME OF CHAOS

Coincidentally, 1959, when Mircioiu and Cho moved to Pyongyang, was a time intertwined with major historical events, including the repatriation of North Korean war orphans.

In Eastern Europe, it was a period in which North Korean students, influenced by the anti-Soviet liberalization movement, sought asylum. It was a time when maneuvers were plotted to remove Kim Il Sung from power and Kim's loyalists acted to stop them. In 1959, Kim locked the doors to the outside world and started a nationwide crackdown. It was also a period in which North Korea started establishing the *Juche ideology*, based on the idolization of Kim. The lives of two ordinary people were swept into the whirlwind of history. North Korea's bid to escape Soviet and Chinese influence while emphasizing national self-reliance eventually led to isolation.

This made the North Korean economy even worse off. The first notable change was that food rations to the residents began to shrink. Mircioiu, who lived in Pyongyang, felt this acutely.

"I had a ration card, so I was given 500 grams of rice for men and 300 grams for women (in my household) per day. Meat rations were available once a month—about half a kilogram, which only served one person. They were only available to special people, so they weren't available

on the market.
Ordinary people could only see meat about three times a year. As I remember, I only ate meat three times: May 1, Labor Day; August 15, Liberation Day; and January 1, New Year's Day."

— Georgeta Mircioiu

As the economy worsened, so did the atmosphere in Pyongyang. Food became scarce, and the locals began to eye foreigners more warily. Mircioiu also began to sense a shift in attitudes. The uncle who kindly kissed the back of her hand, as well as her neighbors and the colleagues she met at university—they all began to look at her with strange, vigilant eyes.

"Life was hard. My colleagues asked me why I lived in North Korea and not Romania. It was so poor that every day, I had to eat chestnut porridge, made by crushing chestnuts and mixing them with milk.
Even though the people who were selected as public agents were college students or ordinary people, they had to go out and work in the fields during the sowing season. One job was to level the ground. One man was carrying a backpack, and the man behind him was picking rocks up from the ground and putting them in.
Someone came and told me, 'Work there.' But I said, 'I do not have North Korean citizenship, and I do not want to work like that.' It was such a bad situation."

— Georgeta Mircioiu

In such unfavorable conditions, Mircioiu became pregnant. The economic situation in North Korea was hardly conducive to having and raising children: after her child was born, she could not properly obtain even a single piece of cloth, let alone clothes for her newborn.

Mircioiu and daughter Miran Cho, 1961.

Mircioiu decided to return to Bucharest for several months to give birth and take care of her child.

On December 22, 1960, a daughter, Miran Cho, was born to Georgeta Mircioiu and Cho Chung Ho. The daughter was named by her father. She was named 'Miran,' representing a beautiful bridge between Korea and Romania. Mircioiu returned to Bucharest for a while and worked there as a temporary teacher. But she couldn't live apart from her husband. She wanted to return to Pyongyang. Mircioiu held her daughter to her chest and took her passport photo. She went to the North Korean embassy in Romania and applied for a visa to visit North Korea. And a few months later, on a cold winter day in early 1961, she once again boarded the train to Pyongyang, this time with her infant daughter in her arms.

EXCLUSION CAMPAIGN

In 1961, the situation in North Korea was far worse than when she first came. The first people to be restricted were foreigners. Though North Korea claims to treat all people equally, in reality it is a very discriminatory class society. Only the *Baekdu bloodline*, which started with Kim Il Sung's band of anti-Japanese guerrillas, and the Nakdong-gang bloodline, which started with Korean War soldiers, are given the full set of privileges. This emphasis on bloodlines began in the early 1960s.

Since then, there have been cases when mixed Korean/foreign couples were forced to separate or divorce. To do this, the government typically assigned the North Korean partner to a remote North Korean province. That was what happened to Cho Chung Ho.

> "There was no consideration for foreigners
> in Pyongyang, and people who were not members of
> the national political party could not even be in
> Pyongyang. Cho Chung Ho was a member of the political
> party, but due to various changes in the situation, he was
> assigned to be a provincial teacher.
> Compared to Pyongyang, the environment in
> the provinces was poor. He even said that he slept at his
> desk in the school office because he had nowhere to live.

Even the boarding house he barely got a place in was in poor condition. He said that one day, a woman was lying in the bed where he was supposed to be. In 1961, strange things were happening, and it was sad in many ways."
— Georgeta Mircioiu

A campaign to exclude foreigners, centered on monitoring and discriminating against foreigners, emerged. Even diplomatic missions were wiretapped and threats made against them. Significantly, the campaign to exclude foreigners occurred at the same time as North Korea began establishing the Juche ideology. Innocent foreigners were treated like criminals. During this period, all remaining North Korean war orphans in Eastern Europe were repatriated.

Distressing days continued for Mircioiu. Her daughter, Miran, suddenly fell ill and started vomiting blood. Mircioiu rushed her to the hospital, but doctors could not ascertain the cause. The disease, it was later discovered, was caused by malnutrition. But there was no way to cure it in North Korea.

"I couldn't stay in North Korea any longer, because Cho Chung Ho had moved to another city, and I had to live alone in Pyongyang with our child. Even our living expenses were not supported from anywhere.
I had to pay rent for an apartment, and I needed to pay for my living expenses, but there was no financial support. Literally, I had to endure the hardships day by day."
— Georgeta Mircioiu

DEPORTATION AND FORCED SEPARATION

Mircioiu and Cho's relationship and marriage and their difficult life in Pyongyang and long-term separation seem like part of a huge historical drama. The life of Mircioiu, who risked everything for love in a desperate situation of war and destruction, death and survival, was entangled with modern Korean history.

It is rare for so many historical events to intersect in the life of one individual. As North Korea began to isolate itself, the resulting changes shattered the peaceful lives of Mircioiu and Cho.

> "They (the North Koreans) started to see foreign women who were married to North Korean husbands differently. Sometimes they thought we were not chaste women. We were discriminated against and subject to surveillance simply because we were foreigners.
> When I met and helped North Korea with Cho Chung Ho, who had brought war orphans, I thought of Romania and North Korea not as countries foreign to each other, but as brothers.
> But the North Koreans didn't seem to think of me that way. I think the *Juche ideology* changed people's thinking."
> — Georgeta Mircioiu

North Korea's relations with the Soviet Union and China became more distant, daily necessities became scarce. As a result, many people had to carry out manual labor while being housed in tents. Because Mircioiu was a foreigner, she was never mobilized for forced labor. But the situation was different for Cho. As a senior official in the Ministry of Education, his position was precarious, simply because he had a foreign wife.

And indeed, one day, Cho was dismissed and reassigned to the provinces—as a coal mine worker. Meanwhile, Mircioiu had to stay in Pyongyang and raise her daughter by herself. Her life was an ongoing battle with hunger and fear. At that time, North Korea was trying to suppress the unsuccessful pro-Soviet and pro-China plot to replace Kim Il Sung. People who were inclined to foreign ideas or came from abroad were subject to surveillance.

At the same time, the North Korean government began forcing those of its citizens with foreign spouses to leave them. Banners praising Kim Il Sung or promoting national self-reliance were hung above the streets.

Diplomatically, North Korea began pursuing a line independent of the Soviet Union and China. This naturally meant distancing itself from the communist parties of Eastern Europe. In particular, the Hungarian Revolution, which advocated liberalization, and the mass protests in Poland were a potential threat to Kim Il Sung's rule in North Korea. This was why the regime intensified its ideological control over the North Korean population in this period.

By 1962, all the North Korean college students and technical trainees based in the five Eastern European countries were withdrawn. A vast curtain began to surround North Korea. In this atmosphere, foreigners like Mircioiu could no longer live in Pyongyang.

"When I walked down the street, many people looked at foreigners and scowled. I had to buy a train ticket to meet my husband, but I didn't have enough money, so I had to pawn my winter coat at a pawn shop.
At the pawn shop, they said they were checking my identity with my fingerprints. I felt very bad, because I had never had my fingerprints taken.
The situation had changed from when I first entered Korea, and the atmosphere in the 1960s had already changed. In 1959, the atmosphere of care and respect for us disappeared."

— Georgeta Mircioiu

Food, including rice, was being rationed, and even then it was not distributed normally. Openness toward foreigners disappeared, and those North Koreans who did not belong to the Workers' Party of Korea were forced to leave Pyongyang. Mircioiu had to make a decision. Should she stay in North Korea with her husband, or leave to get treatment for their ill daughter?

Cho was pragmatic. He felt that curing their daughter's illness was the top priority. He also felt it would not be easy for his wife to live alone with her young daughter in an unstable North Korea, where economic hardship and discrimination against foreigners were getting worse.

Finally, Mircioiu and Cho decided to leave North Korea together. At the time, they didn't think they would have any problem doing so. After all, they were a legally recognized couple and, with their daughter, a family. Citing the need to get treatment for his sick daughter, Cho applied to the North Korean authorities for permission to leave the country. However, the authorities turned down the request. They said Cho was a "person needed by the party."

After much deliberation, Mircioiu and Cho decided the only option was for Mircioiu to take their daughter to Romania to treat her illness there. Mircioiu was upset about having to part from her husband. Cho tried to comfort her, saying: "I will invite you back to North Korea as soon as Miran recovers. Don't worry, I can move to Romania if things get bad."

> "There were many times when I told my husband that we should go back to Romania to live. Each time, my husband's answer was always the same. 'My country sent me here, and I have to work and live for my country. Someday, when the time is right, we'll go abroad and live together.'
> In hindsight, I think my husband already knew by then that he could not leave North Korea. He knew, so he said what he said to convince me. I was well aware that I could no longer live there with my daughter as a foreigner.
> We all wanted to leave North Korea and live a safe life. My husband, Cho Chung Ho, was that kind of person."
> — Georgeta Mircioiu

LAST FAMILY PHOTO

A few days before Mircioiu left Pyongyang, Cho suddenly asked her to take a commemorative photo. Mircioiu was surprised at the request—it was out of character for Cho. Mircioiu vividly remembers the day their last family photo was taken. She and Cho walked down the streets of Pyongyang, where the spring sun was shining warmly. Holding the hand of their three-year-old daughter, Miran, who had just started walking, the two headed to the photo studio.

On that day, Cho left the house in a particularly neat suit and tie. As he walked to the photo studio, Cho was silent. Later that day, his expression became even darker. The three of them sat down in front of the camera. Mircioiu never imagined that it would be their last family portrait.

For Mircioiu, April 29, 1962, was an unforgettable day. That was the day Mircioiu left Pyongyang with her daughter. Her husband saw them off at Pyongyang Train Station. Cho hugged his daughter tightly and kissed her forehead. Miran waved goodbye to her father without understanding why they were parting. Cho took Mircioiu's hand and hugged her affectionately. That was the last time Mircioiu saw her husband.

Cho Chung Ho, Mircioiu, and daughter Miran in their last family photo, taken in Pyongyang in 1962.

"My husband came aboard the train to get me a seat. And he asked a man sitting next to us to take good care of us. Tears came to my eyes the moment I heard that. I couldn't even hold back my tears. I continued to weep until we crossed the border between North Korea and China. People in the train car came and comforted me.
As the train passed through China, it stopped briefly at a station. When the train slowly began to move again, my daughter, Miran, suddenly got up and shouted loudly out the window: 'There's my dad. Why doesn't Dad get on the train?' She saw a Chinese man standing on the platform. To her, the man looked like her father."
— Georgeta Mircioiu

The moment she parted from her husband at the Pyongyang Train Station more than 60 years ago was etched in Mircioiu's memory. As the train began to move, belching smoke, the figure of her husband waving to the train gradually faded into the distance. That day, Cho had a gut feeling that that moment might be their last one together. That was why he wanted to have a family photo taken. Returning to Romania, Mircioiu received a letter from her husband.

> "The day after you left for Romania, I went to Sinsan (in South Hamgyong Province). I am no longer an intellectual but a manual worker. A member of the working class who has to work in the coal mines. But I'm not sad. Because I have you and our daughter, Miran."
> — Cho Chung Ho, in a letter to Mircioiu

Cho Chung Ho was targeted for being married to a foreigner and for potentially having an individualistic ideology, because he had lived in Europe for a long time. Thus, his dream of living his whole life for his country, party, and family was shattered. That was how it was in North Korea in the early 1960s.

DEATH OF CHO CHUNG HO

After returning to Romania, Mircioiu was reinstated as a teacher at the school where she had taught. Life in Romania was more comfortable than it had been in North Korea. But she was never at ease with the fact that she had had to leave her husband behind. One fortunate thing was that Miran fully recovered from her illness and grew up healthy.

> "When we came back to Romania, Miran turned three years old. She was a smart kid, so she was good at speaking up in kindergarten and grew up to be a beautiful girl. I remember when she was four years old and I went to the North Korean embassy in Bucharest to apply for a visa to enter North Korea. Miran was apparently taught in social studies class at school to say, 'This is Romania and we are Romanians.' An official at the North Korean embassy asked Miran, 'What country are you from?' Miran replied, 'I'm Romanian,' just as she had learned at school. Then the North Korean official said, 'Yeah? Why do Romanians want to go to North Korea? You should stay here in Romania.'"
>
> — Georgeta Mircioiu

Georgeta Mircioiu, a Romanian woman who has been waiting for her North Korean husband for over 60 years.

In the end, mother and daughter were not allowed to enter North Korea. Mircioiu stayed in Romania and continued corresponding with her husband by letter. The news that Cho Chung Ho, who had been hospitalized before marriage due to pneumonia, was now working in a coal mine made Mircioiu even more sad. And she kept trying to go back to North Korea or bring her husband to Romania. However, to do so, she would first have to get permission from the North Korean authorities.

If the North Korean authorities continued to obstruct Cho's journey to Romania, he had the option of trying to escape from North Korea. However, Cho was against such a move. Cho was a proud intellectual, a socialist, and patriotic toward his country.

The couple kept in touch via letters, hoping that one day their family could be reunited. Then one day, a letter arrived from an unfamiliar sender. The letter stated that Cho had gone missing. For Mircioiu, it felt like the sky had caved in.

"I ran to the North Korean embassy in Romania to find out the exact circumstances of my husband's disappearance. But I was told only that my husband, Cho Chung Ho, had gone missing.
'What do you mean?' I said, and the man there told me to come back in a month. So I went back a month later, and this time he said, 'Your husband is dead.' Hearing that, I was so shocked I nearly fainted.
'Then just let me find the remains of my husband,' I demanded. But the North Korean authorities did not allow me to enter. I wasn't even told why North Korea refused me entry. I just couldn't stand it.
After that, I went to the Geneva Human Rights Commission and asked for help. Through the embassies of several countries, including Australia and Singapore, I asked North Korea to confirm whether my husband was alive or dead. However, Pyongyang did not reply to anyone."

— Georgeta Mircioiu

UNRESOLVED QUESTIONS

How did this happen to Mircioiu? Why did her husband, Cho Chung Ho, suddenly disappear? And why, even 60 years later, is it still impossible to confirm whether he is alive or dead? To better understand the situation, I visited Izydor Urian. He had served as Romanian ambassador to Seoul in the 1990s. Before that, he had been the Romanian ambassador to Pyongyang.

I first met Ambassador Urian while researching Mircioiu's story in 2004. Ambassador Urian, too, could not help but be affected by the passing of 15 years. He had recently suffered a stroke and had barely survived. Because of that, he found it difficult to move, and some things he was unable to remember. Despite his physical hardships, Ambassador Urian readily accepted my request for an interview. Perhaps he thought this might be the last time he could recount Mircioiu's story.

As a diplomat, he worked according to the motto "Pursue harmony, but do not be swept away by the crowd." Thus he pursued his interests as a diplomat without allowing anything to interfere.

Fifteen years ago, he had provided useful information on Mircioiu and Cho Chung Ho's case. I came to see him again to reconfirm the account he had given back then.

Because Ambassador Urian had lived in both Seoul and Pyongyang, he understood well the history of the division of the

Izydor Urian, a former Romanian ambassador to Pyongyang, whom I met in Bucharest during my 2004 research.

Korean peninsula. In addition, he knew in detail the obstacles Mircioiu had faced in seeking Cho. In fact, he even tried to contact the North Korean Ministry of Foreign Affairs through various channels to resolve this matter. In 1971, when Romanian president Ceaușescu visited Kim Il Sung in Pyongyang, Ambassador Urian formally raised the issue of Mircioiu and Cho.

> "The Romanian government officially requested confirmation as to whether Cho Chung Ho was alive or dead. Since the marriage was approved by the two governments, official confirmation was required even for divorce. North Korean authorities repeatedly made conflicting statements about whether Cho Chung Ho was alive or dead. I didn't know which words to believe. While this situation continued, Ceaușescu made an official visit to North Korea in 1971, and we formally requested confirmation through diplomatic channels of whether Cho Chung Ho was alive or dead. The problem is that Cho Chung Ho, who was (supposedly) dead at that time, appeared in public."
>
> — Izydor Urian, former Romanian ambassador to North Korea

There were several reasons why the North Korean authorities revealed Cho Chung Ho's appearance. First of all, it seems that they did not want to offend Romanian president Ceaușescu, who was very close to Kim Il Sung. Romania was the country that provided the most support and aid among the countries maintaining diplomatic relations with North Korea in the 1950s. Diplomatically, it would have been awkward for Kim Il Sung to reject Romania's inquiry out of hand.

Another reason was to appease Mircioiu, who was constantly requesting confirmation of Cho Chung Ho's status through international human rights groups. By showing that Cho was alive and well, they were implying that Mircioiu should stop searching for him.

> "Sometimes they said he went missing. At some point (they said) he died. And sometimes they said they needed him for the party. I've seen his date of death and other information change over time, for the sake of the party. Seeing that, I could no longer trust the North Korean regime. Obviously, I knew something bad was happening to my husband."
> — Georgeta Mircioiu

After that, Mircioiu continued to send out letters trying to find Cho. She also wrote letters to Cho's hometown and to his relatives and his brothers in Hamgyong-namdo Province. However, she received no news about Cho.

In 1977, the letters Mircioiu had written were sent back to her. This had not happened before and implied that the addressee could no longer be found. It was the beginning of her despair.

"The last letter I received was when my husband, Cho Chung Ho, was working in a coal mine. A man working in a coal mine came to his house once every three years, and the only place he could come back to change his clothes was his older brother, Mr. Cho Young Ho. He said that Cho got an apartment in Hamheung and left after being assigned to be an engineering professor.

That was the last address where I could send a letter to Cho Chung Ho. I heard that his mother lived with him at the time.

Rather than the post office delivering letters door to door, there was a system in which apartment managers received the letters and distributed them door to door.

"I don't know if the letter was properly delivered after that. Anyway, at that moment, all hope seemed to be in vain, as the letter I had sent to my husband was returned.

"It was a desperate moment. At that time, who could I share my sad feelings with? I had to hide the fact. I couldn't even tell my family that the letter I had sent to my husband had come back."

— Georgeta Mircioiu

EUROPEAN WOMEN WAITING FOR THEIR HUSBANDS

In a normal society, it is unconscionable for the state to forcibly separate loved ones. It is even more unconscionable for the state to force couples to divorce just because one of them is a foreigner.

However, all of this was done in North Korea in the 1960s. North Korea's ideology of excluding foreigners is connected with its ideology of racial purity. It is similar to the xenophobia of all totalitarian countries. The racial purity of the Aryan race advocated by the Nazis while persecuting Jews and the ideology of racial purity advocated by North Korea when it reinforced the *Juche ideology* and rejected foreigners are different only in timing and form; the fundamentals are the same.

In the 1960s, North Korea was already closing its doors to the world. The authorities could have simply issued a departure permit for mixed North Korean / foreign couples. However, those authorities did not want North Koreans and foreigners living as couples even abroad. For the regime, maintaining its control over people was a top priority. The goal was to create a society in which everyone was loyal to Kim Il Sung and Kim Il Sungism was the only ideology.

Halina Ogarek-Czoj, who founded the first Korean language department at the University of Warsaw, also married a North Korean man and had a daughter in Pyongyang before being deported. While living in Poland, Ogarek-Czoj never remarried and waited anxiously for the return of her North Korean husband. However, she died without receiving any news from North Korea.

Polish leader Wojciech Jaruzelski made an official visit to North Korea in 1986. Ogarek-Czoj served as an interpreter at the event where the official meeting between Jaruzelski and Kim Il Sung was held. It was a special move to give her a chance to ask about her husband. Towards the end of the summit, Ogarek-Czoj begged Kim Il Sung to let her see her husband just once. Next to her was Jaruzelski, wordlessly looking on. Kim just listened to her silently. Although she had accompanied the Polish leader as an official interpreter, her heartbreaking wish was not granted.

The foreign women who were forcibly deported from North Korea at the time found that the North Korean regime used various methods to separate them from their husbands. They made the husbands work in another area, and if the foreign wives did not agree to divorce, they did not receive rice rations. Almost all of the foreign wives were forced to leave North Korea. There was no explanation as to why they had to break up or why the family had to be separated.

All they had done was meet and fall in love with North Korean men and marry them. It broke my heart. What country and what system would obstruct family reunions? Could anything in this world take precedence over heartfelt human love? In that sense, the 1960s were both the most innocent and the most brutal of times.

Currently, about 10 European women are known to be waiting to reunite with their North Korean husbands. For them, Korea is not simply a divided country but a country that has torn apart loved ones.

"I don't think it will be easy to forgive North Korea. The education they give always puts the country over the individual. It was that way in the past, and it is still the same today. The first priority is to live for the country and the second priority is to live for the party. The family comes last.
However, the state or party they speak of only means obedience to the Kim Il Sung dynasty. Because of that, my husband was also sacrificed, and I think that I also lead an unhappy life. That is why I cannot forgive North Korea."

CANDLES FOR THE LIVING

In Romania, churchgoers wishing to pray for people light two candles: one for the living and one for the dead. Even now, whenever Georgeta Mircioiu goes to church, she prays for her husband. She lights a candle in the hope that her husband will be able to return to her. The candle she lights for her husband is not for the dead. It is a candle for the living.

Mircioiu's religious beliefs include the notion that souls cannot be reconnected after death. This is why Mircioiu so desperately wants to be reunited with her husband. She believes that her relationship with him exists only in this life. Fifteen years ago, I filmed a scene in which she lit a candle for her husband in the backyard of a small church in Bucharest.

Though years have passed, she still lights a candle once a week to pray for her husband to return to his family. If alive, Cho Chung Ho would be 94 years old. Though the average human lifespan has increased considerably, the chances are low that someone could live beyond the age of 90 in a country with an underdeveloped medical system such as North Korea's. Moreover, her husband had been in poor health from a young age.

Other people in her situation might have given up and started a new life, but Mircioiu has stood by her commitment to her husband. Her love is simply amazing.

One day, I carefully asked her, "Did you ever think about forgetting Cho Chung Ho and meeting another man?" After hearing the question, Mircioiu quietly took a gold ring from off her finger. It was the ring her husband gave her when they got married in 1957. She had never stopped wearing it. Mircioiu handed me the ring and told me to look at the inside. I could see tiny, faint writing engraved on the inside of the ring. To read it, I borrowed the magnifying glass she used to write the dictionary. The inscription read: "1957, Chung Ho."

In the Romanian Orthodox Church, two candles are lit: one for the living and one for the dead. Two stands, one to pray for the "living" (left) and the other for the "dead" (right).

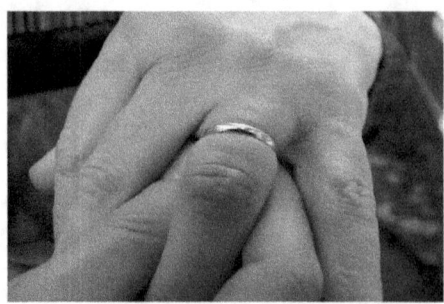

A wedding ring with the words "1957, Chung Ho" engraved on the inside. Ever since she got married, Mircioiu has worn this ring.

It was an ordinary ring with no jewelry or decorations.

In the 1950s, Romania's economic situation was not good, so the couple couldn't afford to buy a ring for each of them. Even buying one was not easy. Mircioiu told her husband, "I don't need a ring," but Cho Chung Ho still wanted to give her one. He also had this simple gold band engraved to symbolize his heartfelt feelings.

TO GIGI

"Romanian women do not take off their wedding rings unless they are divorced. Even when I die, I will still wear the ring. Even if the husband dies, the wedding ring is not removed. As long as you have a loved one, the ring remains on your finger."

— Georgeta Mircioiu

After a while, Mircioiu took an old photo out of an album and showed it to me. On the back of the photo was a message in faded ballpoint pen. It was from Cho, expressing his joy for his love with Mircioiu after the challenges of their secret relationship.

"To Gigi (Cho Chung Ho's nickname for Mircioiu)
March 1, 1953 – March 1, 1955
These two glorious years were truly full of happiness, sadness, and joy. But we won the struggle. Let us move forward more vigorously for the noble fruit we promised each other! I send this for your health, for your joy,
to the one I love the most.
From Chung Ho on March 1, 1955"

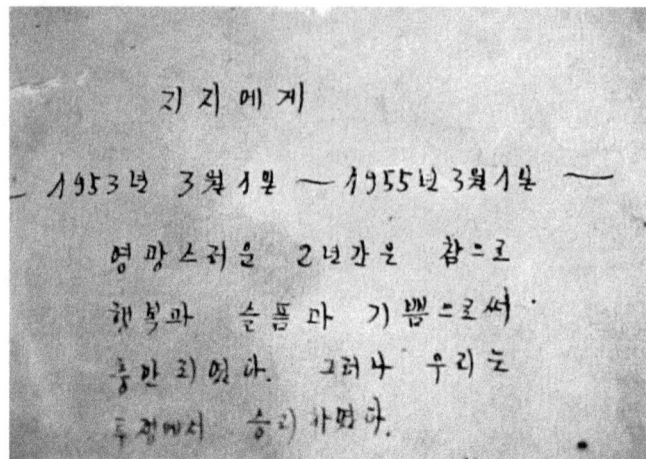

A letter from Cho Chung Ho to Mircioiu.

Cho Chung Ho's writings show the temperament of a North Korean man with a strong socialist ideology. In his letters, he always gave meaning to time by specifying the specific period when he wrote the letter.

Cho was a well-organized and meticulous person. When the couple parted in Pyongyang, he was 36 and Mircioiu was 28. It is said that time heals all wounds, but that was not how Mircioiu experienced it. She endured those long, long separations only by clinging to the hope that she could one day meet her husband.

> "Even if I met my husband right now, I could still recognize him. I still clearly remember his dark hair and his smile. Our daughter resembles her father when she smiles. Sadly, he must have lived his whole life not knowing that his daughter had his smile, right?"
> — Georgeta Mircioiu

Mircioiu's life begins and ends with Cho Chung Ho. In the turbulent 1950s, Cho, who started off as just a stranger from a distant country, became, and has since remained, a big part of her life.

One day, she will depart this world, but I hope that she will be reunited with her husband before then. Even if her wish does not come true, I hope it will always be remembered that there was a woman in Romania who spent her life eagerly waiting for her North Korean husband to return.

I faced many difficulties while doing research in Eastern Europe, but my determination to finish this documentary was because of people like Mircioiu. I needed to tell the world their story.

FLOWER BASKET—IT'S PRETTY!

On February 15, 2019, before I left Romania, I wanted to see Mircioiu one last time. On that day, we filmed her on a walkabout as she shared memories of the places she had often visited with her husband in the 1950s. Many of her memories were thus preserved.

It was the road she took with her husband to submit the marriage application. It was also the road she took when desperately asking for help to find her husband in North Korea. All the stories in her complicated life seemed to involve that same road.

It was sunny and warm that day, as winter was over and spring was about to begin. Romanians celebrate the beginning of spring with the Mărțișor custom. You confess your love to someone by presenting them with a small ornament—usually to wear—which is also called a Mărțișor. It is made by twisting together a red thread, which symbolizes blood and life and a white thread, which symbolizes the innocence of the first buds blooming in spring.

The relationship between Mircioiu and Cho Chung Ho also began with the Mărțișor celebration. Cho's simple statement that day—"Countries have borders, but our friendship has no borders"—moved Mircioiu's heart. After that, she never gave her husband another Mărțișor ornament, but whenever spring came and Mărțișor ornaments appeared on the streets of Bucharest, Mircioiu thought of him. She could not forget the memories of Mărțișor. It was a token of the love that connected her and Cho. She could hardly believe that nearly 70 years had passed since the first gift of Mărțișor to her husband in 1951.

Korean interpreter Won Yoo-sook was with Mircioiu during the filming. She had been helping her for a long time. She also held a small Mărțișor ornament in her hand. It was brought to Mircioiu as a gift. When receiving the Mărțișor adorned with red flowers as a gift, Mircioiu smiled brightly. In Korean, she said:

"Flower basket—it's pretty!"

She said "It's pretty" with a strong North Korean accent. The moment I heard that, it hit home that she really had lived in Pyongyang for two years. Her Korean came out of nowhere, but it somehow made her seem more familiar. She smiled and told us a story.

> "When I was in high school, a psychic came to my house. We had five siblings, and I deliberately turned my head away so the psychic could not see my face and tell my future. Then, just for a moment, I made eye contact with the psychic. He looked at my face and said, 'Your birthday is August 15.' Everyone in the family was surprised. He was right. And he continued by saying, 'You're going to another country, you're going to marry a foreigner, and you're going to have a daughter.' Hearing this, the whole family laughed. 'What kind of foreigner are you marrying?' But looking back, none of the psychic's words were wrong. It seems that I had a certain destiny. Mărțișor was a fateful motif for me."

A photo taken when I visited Romania to film Kim Il Sung's Children. Won Yoo-sook (a Korean volunteer who was helping Georgeta Mircioiu), Georgeta Mircioiu, and the author.

I asked her, "If you had one last wish, what would it be?" She pondered for a moment before answering.

"It is my wish to have my husband by my side. I still want to see that person. I wish I was right next to him right now."

Mircioiu was unable to speak any more. She could no longer hold back her tears and started crying. Her longing for her husband, which the interviews over the past few days had brought to the surface, and the sadness she had had to endure while raising her daughter on her own, burst out all at once. Watching her made me pensive as well. After a while, as she wiped her tears away with a handkerchief, I spoke to her. There was one thing I wanted to ask her.

Did you ever converse with your husband in Korean?
"Yes. Sometimes we talked in Korean."
Please tell me what your husband said at that time that you remember best.

For a moment, Mircioiu pondered the question. As she usually did while contemplating, she put her hand under her chin. She gazed into the air, then turned back to the camera and started to smile.

"I remember. There is one Korean word he used that struck me the most and that he used frequently. When he said that, he looked at me directly. I liked that he said it in Korean. He always said this to me when he started talking. 'My dear….' That word comes to mind now."

FATHER, BE STRONG!

Before we conclude Mircioiu's story, there is one character who cannot be left out: her daughter, Miran Cho. As Mircioiu was without her husband, her daughter Miran became the center of her world. Miran also had to overcome the sadness of having a missing father. The existence of a father in childhood was painful for Miran, who had an Asian father, who also came from North Korea, a country that is poor, far away, and unknown. Watching her daughter grow every year carrying such pain, Mircioiu also had to endure the unbearable sadness.

However, her daughter Miran overcame adversity and did her best in life. Since childhood, she had demonstrated the same intelligence as her father. After graduating from the University of Bucharest, Miran served as the chief secretary of the Romanian delegation to the European Union (EU). Not just anyone could ascend to such a position.

> "When Miran was in college, there was no Korean language department. Instead, there were Chinese and Japanese departments. Miran majored in Chinese and French so that she could talk to her father when he returned. My husband speaks a little Japanese and can write Chinese characters. Miran thought that when her

father came back, the two of them would need to be able to communicate while living together, so Miran studied Chinese. Miran also studied hard and earned the highest possible scores on her college entrance exams."
— Georgeta Mircioiu

My interview with Miran did not go easily, mainly because she insisted on not being involved in anything related to her father. She no longer has her heart set on finding him.

When she was younger, Miran Cho, just like her mother, actively appealed to the international community for her father's release from North Korea. Then came an event she will never forget. In 1994, South Korean newspapers and broadcasts reported that a man had just fled North Korea. His name was Cho Chang Ho. In the Roman alphabet, there was only one letter's difference between that name and her father's name, Cho Chung Ho. The reports spread to Romania, and Miran thought that the man in the news had to be her father.

"At that time, my daughter shouted with joy, saying, 'Finally, my father has found us and escaped from North Korea.' You can't imagine how excited she was. But later, she was very disappointed to hear that it was not Cho Chung Ho but someone else by the name of Cho Chang Ho. She didn't even come out of her room for days. From then on, Miran began to hate talking about her father. She's also kept her distance from me. For Miran, the expectations were high, and so was the disappointment."
— Georgeta Mircioiu

When I first came to Romania in 2004 to conduct research, I formally asked Miran for an interview. But she declined. She said she no longer wanted the emotional struggle of thinking of her father. She said she had already given up on finding him. Through her mother, I tried to persuade her to speak with me, but without success.

I had almost given up on ever interviewing Miran. However, on my last day in Romania, I got an unexpected call from Miran, saying that she would speak with me. I hurriedly gathered my gear and went to meet her. She only allowed 10 minutes for the interview. I couldn't hear her whole story in that short time. But I understood how hard it was for her to allow the interview at all. It was a tense moment. Miran arrived with colleagues from the European Union. Her long, dark hair and her face resembled her father more than it did her mother. We exchanged business cards and spoke briefly before starting the interview. There was a frostiness in her voice.

Why did Miran Cho suddenly change her mind and allow the interview? I didn't include this among my questions. Even if I didn't ask, I understood in my heart. Looking for her father was an endless zig-zag between hope and despair. She deliberately tried to erase her father from her heart because she no longer wanted to experience the frustration. But she still had regrets.

Miran took a seat in front of the camera. She had a neat appearance and determined attitude. In that respect, I thought she might have resembled her father. Among Mircioiu's photos of him, there was one picture of him sitting in a chair just as neatly as Miran did and staring straight ahead.

Cho Chung Ho was a proud idealist who dreamed of a socialist paradise on earth. If he is still alive today, what would he say about his past? He would have missed seeing his beloved wife and daughter for the rest of his life. If he has already died, how did he regard North Korea right before he died?

Seeing Miran was like seeing her father. So Miran was once again struggling to keep the last spark of hope alive. I felt so sad for her. At

Miran Cho at the time of her 2004 interview.

the same time, I felt an indescribable sense of responsibility. As the camera focused on her face, she began to speak.

> "My mother has been working all her life battling the North Korean and Romanian governments to find my father. But so far, we haven't gotten any answers."
> — Miran Cho

Miran began with a story about her mother. In 1960, the love between Mircioiu, a Romanian, and Cho Chung Ho, a North Korean, and her birth. Ten years before she was born, the Korean peninsula was in the midst of war. Because of the war, her father came to faraway Romania with 3,000 war orphans under his wing. The sad history of the Korean War connected their destiny.

Miran may well be the only Romanian to have grown up in Pyongyang. Time is fleeting, and Miran, who was three years old when her mother and father had to part, is now in her 60s. Her father gave her the name "Miran" so she would grow up to be a woman who connected Korea and Romania. From an early age, Miran had felt the presence of her father as a faint memory through her mother.

Miran resembles her father in more than just appearance. The letter Miran wrote in 1968, at the age of eight, was written in the same format as the letter her father sent to her mother in 1955. It was Cho Chung Ho's style to write the name of the addressee and the date of the letter at the bottom. At the end of Miran's letter, the sentence "I am sending this for your joy" is just the same as the last letter her father sent to her mother.

> "To my beloved father,
> May 12, 1962 – June 16, 1968
> My mother and I are waiting for you every day, Father.
> I am sending this for your health, for your joy, my dearest one.
> Father, please come back.
> June 16, 1968
> Your daughter Miran, from Bucharest…."

Maybe Miran wanted to write a letter of sadness and regret for the father who she missed, who she wanted to call "Father," and for her mother, who had lived a lonely life without ever doubting that she would meet her husband again.

Miran sent letters to various human rights organizations in which she recounted her father's story. They were heartbreaking letters asking them to confirm whether her father was alive or dead. Thanks to her efforts, international human rights organizations took the lead and asked North Korea for confirmation. However, she was unable to learn anything about her father's fate.

"Father! Mother has thought only of you all her life. I've been fighting and overcoming hardships. I want to see you as soon as possible.
Dear Father!
If there's anything we can do, we'll do it. We will do anything to meet you."
— Miran Cho

Miran was desperately looking for her father. She was determined to do anything to find him. There is no greater sadness in the world than not being able to meet your parent. For Miran, the waiting turned into resentment, and the resentment turned into hatred. In her eyes, North Korea had become an incomprehensible and abnormal country. So she tried to ignore anything that had to do with Korea. And that was why she initially refused to be interviewed.

Hearing her story, I was very sad. Behind the camera, Mircioiu was watching her daughter. Mircioiu's eyes were wet. Though she must have shed countless tears in her life, Mircioiu still cried when the subject of her husband came up.

That was the last time I saw Mircioiu. I thought it was possible that I would never see her again. And the same thought probably occurred to her. When she took a seat in front of the camera, she said she had one last message to give the world.

"I have something to tell you. My life was very difficult.
To get married, I waited three years for the (North Korean) People's Committee to give permission for our marriage. And I made dictionaries so that I would not lose hope that I could meet my husband again. It took me 30 years to make the dictionaries.
Waiting was sometimes painful, but it was also the happiest of times. Because I have never given up on love.

**I want to tell you this. If there is hope, fight and live your life and don't give up! Fight hard for the noble freedom of our humanity!
My life was never a tragedy. Living was worthwhile. I hope you all remember that."**

— Georgeta Mircioiu

This persistent Romanian woman has been waiting for her North Korean husband for 60 years. The message she wanted to convey to the world would never disappear.

CHAPTER 4

1962: THE YEAR NORTH KOREA CLOSED ITS DOORS

KIM IL SUNG'S VISIT TO EASTERN EUROPE IN 1956 AND HIS CLASH WITH FACTIONALISTS

In February 1956, the 20th Congress of the Communist Party of the Soviet Union was held at the Kremlin. Nikita Khrushchev, who had assumed power after Stalin's death in 1953, gave a shocking speech: he criticized Stalin's cult of personality and all the atrocities the secret police carried out to strengthen the dictatorship.

Khrushchev's secret speech, entitled "On the Cult of Personality and Its Consequences," was a poignant critique of the Stalinist communist dictatorship. The Soviet Union and Eastern European communists took this opportunity to switch to collective rule. It was the beginning of the process of de-Stalinization. The rise of Khrushchev soon led to a liberation movement in Eastern Europe—the October 1956 Hungarian Revolution.

It was at this time that opposition to Kim Il Sung began to emerge within North Korea. The Soviet faction, which backed prioritizing heavy industry (especially military industry) and opposed the cult of personality, and Kim's loyalists, who called for the development of light industry and supported the cult surrounding Kim, collided head-on.

It was at this time that the Soviet faction and the pro-China Yan'an faction were purged. This was an indication that the absolute dictatorship of Kim Il Sung was beginning.

In 1956, Kim Il Sung embarked on a tour of five Eastern European countries. At the same time, inside North Korea, some politicians were planning to challenge Kim Il Sung's leadership.

In June 1956, Kim visited Eastern Europe, where the North Korean war orphans were staying. However, during his official visit, Kim received intelligence that in North Korea, plans were being hatched to expel him from power.

"In June 1956, Kim Il Sung visited Eastern Europe, including Bulgaria. And at the same time, there was a conflict between factions within North Korea. There was an attempt by pro-China Maoists and pro-Soviet factionalists to overthrow Kim Il Sung's leadership. It was a kind of political coup attempt.
Through this process, Kim Il Sung attempted to establish his own unique ideological system. That was the *Juche ideology*."

— Jordan Baev, Bulgarian historian

Kim Il Sung returned to North Korea. He had already planned to purge Pak Heon-yeong, head of the Southern branch of the Workers' Party of Korea, by holding him accountable for the Korean War. Kim indicted Pak on charges of being an American spy and attempting to overthrow the regime, and he was sentenced to death in 1955.

Kim's next move was against the pro-China Yan'an faction. In August 1956, at the plenary meeting of the Central Committee of the Workers' Party of Korea, the Yan'an faction strongly criticized Kim's monolithic ideology and centralized dictatorship.

However, Kim, who was in control of the Party Central Committee, had a numerical advantage and counterattacked. Starting in September 1956, he expelled some Yan'an factionalists and had them removed from the Party Central Committee. A purge of the pro-Soviet faction followed. In March 1958, Kim Il Sung declared the end of the factions at the first meeting of representatives of the Workers' Party of Korea and formalized the victory of his own side.

In purging the opposition, Kim also had to completely revise North Korea's diplomatic line, in which the country depended on the Soviet Union and China. The anti-factionalist campaign was the biggest single step moving North Korea toward an isolationist, monolithic dictatorship. The regime banned and destroyed all books that did not support Kim's monolithic ideological system. To purge the opposition, Kim set up political prison camps. Politicians from the Yan'an faction and the Soviet faction, fearful of Kim's bloody purge, applied for asylum in China and the Soviet Union, respectively.

As a result, Kim Il Sung completely suppressed the forces that challenged his leadership. He also used this as an opportunity to strengthen his one-man dictatorship and establish a North Korean-style leader system. To this end, the *Juche ideology* was established in North Korean society. The anti-factionalism campaign was a great victory for Kim Il Sung and his supporters but a disaster for North Korea as a whole. Although history cannot be based on speculation, if Kim had been defeated in the clash with the factionalists in 1956, the political system in North Korea would not be as closed and distorted as it is today.

DISTORTED SOCIETY

To understand what was going on inside North Korea in the 1960s and 1970s, I interviewed Professor Gábor Osváth of the University of Budapest, Hungary. He studied in North Korea in 1970–1972. He observed directly how the power struggle within North Korea and the cult of personality surrounding Kim Il Sung developed.

According to Professor Osváth, the North Korean state began to take the path of national isolation in 1958–1959. It criticized the Soviet Union and China, from which it received practical support during the Korean War, for their "imperialist" foreign policies, and it began to block foreign influences, especially in art and culture. At the same time, Juche was promoted throughout society.

"If you look at a picture of North Korea taken in 1958, you see that dancers are practicing in ballet shoes. But after 1959, the ballet shoes of dancers suddenly disappeared. I wondered what the reason was. I had a chance to meet the North Korean ambassador, and I asked, 'Why don't the dancers wear ballet shoes?' I got a ridiculous excuse. It was that 'ballet shoes do not fit the body of North Korean women.' That was a silly answer.

There were no Western musical instruments to be found either. At this time, they started making stringed

Professor Gábor Osváth, who lived in North Korea in the early 1970s, and a North Korean official at the University of Budapest, Hungary.

instruments such as the violin, the cello, the viola, and the contrabass. Even Western-style strollers disappeared from the streets of Pyongyang. The women were all carrying their children on their backs."
— Professor Gábor Osváth, University of Budapest, Hungary

Censorship began to be applied to views of history. According to Professor Osváth, mentioning unofficial interpretations of history became dangerous.

"At that time, in North Korea, you could only find books that praised Kim Il Sung for his partisan activities. Most of the books published in the West had disappeared. Talking about history was treason, and I felt uncomfortable about giving economic aid abroad to help North Korea.
The only (history) books that were published were those containing anecdotes to inspire North Korean pride.

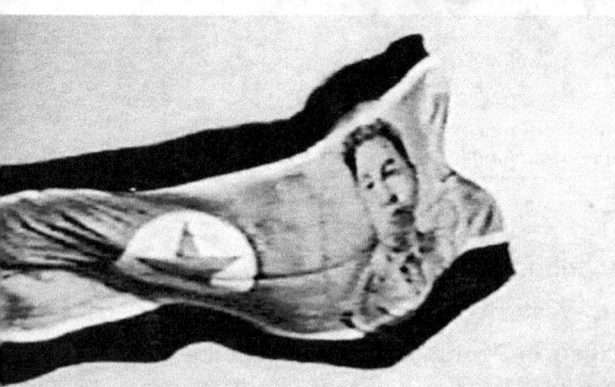

A newsreel found in Romania vividly records the morning assemblies of North Korean war orphans. (Top photo) A North Korean flag bearing the portrait of Kim Il Sung. Siret, Romania, 1953. (Bottom photo)

The achievements of Kim Il Sung were celebrated everywhere."

— Professor Gábor Osváth

After the Korean War, many foreign countries stepped in to help North Korea, which was damaging to North Korea's pride.

At the same time, the cult of personality surrounding Kim Il Sung was constructed. The *Juche ideology* started by glorifying and mythologizing Kim's anti-Japanese guerrilla struggle. It was a largely fabricated history.

Historical anecdotes also appeared one after another to inspire North Korea's pride. Foreigners and foreign cultures were unconditionally excluded. There was even a proposal to take down the monuments built to commemorate the Soviet soldiers who died liberating northern Korea from the Japanese in World War II and the Chinese soldiers who died defending North Korea in the Korean War. Ultimately, the plan was not carried out due to opposition from China and the Soviet Union. Nevertheless, Kim Il Sung's own achievements were now celebrated everywhere. Ordinary families were instructed to hang a framed portrait of Kim on the wall in their homes. The idolization of Kim began while he was alive.

Some North Korean researchers argue that, because of its special situation, North Korea inevitably required an ideological consciousness for internal unity, such as the *Juche ideology*. It is argued that North Korea's closed political system was an inevitable response of self-defense due to the U.S. economic and military blockade. However, this argument is less convincing when considering the indoctrination of North Korean war orphans in Eastern Europe.

It is more persuasive to conclude that North Korea was already built around Kim Il Sung from the time the state was formed. Indeed, to this day, 34,000 statues of Kim stand throughout North Korea.

> "Eastern Europe, although under Soviet influence, differed from country to country. In East Germany, for example, the Stasi (secret police) played a major role in maintaining the political system, but a cult of personality was not created as it was in North Korea. Communism is not the same everywhere.
> In the case of North Korea, in order to strengthen Kim Il Sung's monolithic ideology system, political enemies were purged, and the censorship of books and ideological control over the people were strengthened. The problem is that as Kim Il Sungism was strengthened, the North Korean economy slowly began to collapse."
> — Gábor Osváth

In the early 1950s, the same morning assembly was held everywhere in Eastern Europe where North Korean war orphans stayed.

Bulgarian historian Jordan Baev interprets this bizarre phenomenon within North Korea from a geopolitical point of view.

> "I believe that these confrontations and conflicts were caused by political and geopolitical factors, not ideological conflicts. It can be understood as a conflict between China and the Soviet Union, which sought to expand its influence in the Third World.
> These political and geopolitical factors are among the decisive factors that made North Korea, which was located between China and the Soviet Union, seek an independent path to survival."
> — Jordan Baev

MASTER OF PURGING AND REMOVAL OF POLITICAL ENEMIES

The Cold War system was bipolar, centered on the United States and the Soviet Union. But in the early 1960s, the struggle for world hegemony was joined by a third power: China. This confrontation continued into the late 1970s. And Kim Il Sung took full advantage of Sino-Soviet rivalry to strengthen his regime. He sought to walk a tightrope between the leading communist nation, the Soviet Union, and fast-emerging China.

Even at the height of the anti-factionalist campaign, there were about 100,000 Chinese troops in North Korea. To Kim Il Sung, their presence was an irritating obstacle to his efforts to walk an independent path. However, Kim could not openly ignore China, which had helped North Korea during the Korean War. In purging the factionalists, Kim focused on the Yan'an faction, supported by China.

Kim Il Sung demonstrated his power by promoting numerous descendants of his anti-Japanese guerrillas into positions of power. This was why his first goal was to eliminate the Southern branch of the Workers' Party of Korea, which had the most members.

More advanced tactics were needed to eliminate the pro-Soviet and pro-China political forces. First of all, Kim Il Sung had his own loyalists take control of the plenary meeting of the Party Central Committee, which served as the national assembly. It was different from the purge of Pak Heon-yeong, a former leader of the Southern branch of the Workers' Party of Korea, on charges of espionage.

At a plenary meeting dominated by Kim Il Sung supporters, the Yan'an faction were dragged off the podium and prevented from giving a proper speech, as the attendees booed and swore at them. It was not a direct purge but a method of eliminating the opposition by the power of the crowd in a public space.

In the heated atmosphere of the conference hall, the members of the Yan'an faction could sense the threat they faced. They left the conference hall, immediately got into cars, and fled to China. Their defection was essentially an admission that they had lost the power struggle with Kim Il Sung.

The same was the case with pro-Soviet figures. Criticism of the cult of personality was denounced as "factionalism" and anti-state activity. Choe Chang-ik, an iconic figure representing the opposition to Kim Il Sung, was purged and spent the rest of his life in a political prison camp. Pak Heon-yeong, the leader of the Southern branch of the Workers' Party of Korea, was sentenced to death and secretly executed.

It was at this time that the infamous North Korean political prison camps first appeared. Political prison camps were used to detain many politicians branded as "counter-revolutionaries" and expelled from office.

> "In the early 1960s, there was a confrontation centered on 'Beijing-Moscow-Washington'; the two major axes were the Soviet Union and the United States. This trend continued into the late 1970s. It was the time when Deng Xiaoping and Nikita Khrushchev each took power. Kim Il Sung used his geopolitical position in the gap between the Soviet Union and China to stabilize his system."
>
> — Jordan Baev, Bulgarian historian

In the end, Kim Il Sung completely suppressed the factionalists, strengthening his one-man dictatorship and establishing a North Korean-style leader system. These were measures to place Kim Il Sung above the state, party, and people. The anti-factionalist campaign paved the way for Kim Il Sung's political victory and long-term rule. However, at that time, few people would have predicted that the Kim family's dynasty would continue for over 70 years. To this day, North Korea still promotes the anti-factionalist campaign as a key step in achieving party unity and moving toward the Juche-oriented socialist construction centering on the party and the leader.

In reality, though, it was a bloody purge that established a semi-civilized and feudal dictatorship that was unprecedented in the world. Starting in the 1950s, North Korea spent an entire decade focusing on idolizing Kim Il Sung. It was the time when North Korea exited the international community and entered a path of self-isolation. As a result, the North Korean economy began to collapse in the 1970s.

If North Korea had not moved toward "self-reliance" in the 1960s and instead stayed more connected with the international community under the banner of socialist internationalism, the fate of the Korean peninsula might have been different. The Eastern bloc's ideal of a fraternal socialist community was what rescued nearly 10,000 war orphans in the 1950s. Since then, however, North Korea has been transformed into a state in which all citizens must obey and sacrifice for Kim Il Sung. North Korean war orphans in Eastern Europe were also victims of that history.

THE HUNGARIAN REVOLUTION

When discussing the North Korean war orphans, one relevant event in world history cannot be overlooked. This was the revolution and fight for freedom that took place in Hungary in 1956. Khrushchev, who took power after Stalin's death in 1953, began to emphasize the collective leadership system while criticizing the Stalinist dictatorship. Amid these changes, a wind of liberalization began to blow in Eastern Europe.

After World War II, communist governments were established in Eastern European countries under Soviet influence. In 1947, the Stalinist Mátyás Rákosi came to power in Hungary. Rákosi, who was known as "Stalin's best pupil," promoted the nationalization of industry and the collectivization of agriculture. In the process, about 7,000 party members who opposed him were purged. As the political turmoil and economic difficulties overlapped, the Hungarian people's dissatisfaction with Rákosi increased.

With Stalin's death in 1953, Rákosi also lost power. A new, reform-oriented government emerged, but Rákosi refused to change and fought the government's policy.

The Hungarian Revolution of 1956 began when the Hungarian people exploded in anger at Rákosi and his fellow hardliners. On October 23, 1956, demonstrators in Budapest, the capital, tore down a statue of Stalin and smashed its head in. Soon, security forces and protesters clashed, resulting in bloodshed.

The situation spiraled out of control as the radio station was taken over by the militia and Soviet troops entered Budapest. On the next day, October 24, a gunfight broke out between the militia and Soviet forces, resulting in many casualties. Soon, as feared, Soviet tanks advanced into Budapest. The militia fought bravely against well-trained Soviet troops and tanks but were defeated by November 11.

In Budapest, protesters hoisted Hungarian flags with the Stalinist-era coat of arms cut out of the middle. From then on, the Hungarian flag with a hole in the middle became known worldwide as a symbol of the country's longing for freedom and its resistance to communist oppression.

During the three weeks of fierce fighting, more than 3,000 people were killed or missing, and more than 20,000 were injured. Half of those who died were manual laborers, and more than half of the casualties were young people under the age of 30.

The Hungarian Revolution started a wind of anti-Soviet liberalization in Eastern Europe. At the same time in Poland, mass protests for freedom took place. The 1968 protest movement in Prague, Czechoslovakia, was greatly influenced by these two events.

Interestingly, a few of the North Korean war orphans and college students who studied in Eastern Europe during this period participated in the Hungarian Revolution. Although they participated as individuals, their involvement was noted by North Korean intelligence and reported to Pyongyang.

North Korea's repatriation of its war orphans and college students was in large part a reaction to the Eastern European liberalization movement. Kim Il Sung was concerned that if the situation was neglected, the spark would spread to North Korean society.

From the perspective of Kim Il Sung, who faced down a leadership challenge, the nearly 10,000 well-educated young people who had directly experienced the winds of liberalization in Eastern Europe risked destabilizing his system.

THE WINDS OF CHANGE IN EASTERN EUROPE

Until 1955, before the wave of anti-Soviet liberalization across Eastern Europe, Kim Il Sung planned to use the North Korean war orphans to improve diplomatic relations with Eastern European countries. In North Korea, core technologies such as coal mining depended on Soviet know-how, and Kim wanted domestic technicians in this industry. That is why in 1955, Kim Il Sung issued direct guidance that the war orphans focus on technical education.

From then on, the most academically promising North Korean children were assigned to attend the same schools as European children. In Hungary, they were sent to technical schools for intensive training. The elite were selected to receive lessons in advanced European technology. For this purpose, 200 war orphans in Poland were relocated to the city of Otwock.

> "In 1955, Kim Il Sung gave orders to move children from Prochowice, Poland, to Otwock, outside Warsaw.
> He thought that sending North Korean children to a Polish school in Otwock, near the Polish capital, to study with Polish children would be an effective way for them to learn the local language and culture.
> In fact, the Polish Ministry of Education even prepared a new educational program to give North Korean and

> Polish children opportunities to interact.
> But in 1956, things changed. Kim Il Sung feared that the sparks of revolution in Hungary and Poland would reach North Korea. So in 1956, he issued an order to repatriate children from Europe to North Korea."
>
> — Sylwia Szyc, Polish researcher of North Korea

Many of the North Korean war orphans who grew familiar with European culture over a long period developed a European mindset. This was particularly the case with children who had come to Eastern Europe when they were very young. They looked like North Koreans, but they felt like Europeans. As they had learned the local language, they freely socialized with Europeans and were able to understand political developments in Europe.

The death of Stalin, who had built a cult of personality around himself, made these North Koreans skeptical of communism. And being exposed to the works of European intellectuals and artists changed their way of thinking.

Starting in early 1956, an unusual atmosphere could be sensed in the dormitories where the North Korean war orphans were staying. Some of the children secretly snuck out of the dormitory and enjoyed the relatively free environment of Eastern Europe. A few of the older ones climbed over the fence and drank alcohol or secretly dated European women.

The news of the Hungarian Revolution changed the children. The children were shocked to hear about the Hungarians fighting for freedom and against dictatorship.

> "In 1956, several North Korean students joined the Hungarian Revolution. Seeing this phenomenon, the North Korean embassy in Budapest decided to repatriate the children to North Korea.

In 1956, Kim Il Sung visited an orphan dormitory in Hungary.

The target group included not only North Korean students and orphans but also technicians. As a result, no North Korean students were officially able to stay in Hungary after 1957."

— Sylwia Szyc, Polish researcher of North Korea

The same thing also happened in Poland and Romania. In May 1957, the North Korean embassy in Poland received an urgent message from the Polish intelligence service. It said that two North Korean students had been caught at a border checkpoint while trying to escape by train to Austria from Prochowice, where the North Korean war orphans were based.

Although the two students who escaped from the dormitory cannot be identified today, documents from the Polish intelligence service establish that these two North Korean war orphans were students living in Prochowice. It was the very place where the dormitories of war orphans from North Korea were located. Two North Korean students were abducted by North Korean agents and eventually forcibly repatriated to North Korea.

ESCAPING THE DORMITORY

In 1956, the Hungarian liberalization wave spread faster than expected in Eastern Europe. The Hungarian Revolution was a great shock to the North Korean war orphans living in Eastern Europe. Resistance to the Soviet Union, the leader of the socialist bloc, and criticism of Stalin, who had been deified, caused them to start doubting the ideas they had been taught.

North Korea's intelligence authorities also strengthened their surveillance system. They were concerned that the Hungarian Revolution would influence North Korean war orphans in Eastern Europe. And what they feared soon became a reality.

In 1957, in Warsaw, Poland, young North Korean college students sent letters to the American and French embassies requesting political asylum. Their letters were intercepted by the Polish intelligence service and eventually forwarded to the North Korean embassy in Poland. All the North Korean college students involved in the incident were abducted, repatriated to North Korea, and sent to political prison camps.

This was the time when Kim Il Sung's regime intensified its anti-Soviet, anti-China policy. It was also a time when power in North Korea was completely taken over by Kim Il Sung loyalists who eradicated the opposition. Kim needed a new ideology to justify his absolute rule. This was the *Juche ideology*.

> "Conflicts began to arise after Stalin's death,
> as the communist system began to change. Khrushchev
> tried to reform the communist bloc. But Kim Il Sung didn't
> want to be part of that bloc. So Kim Il Sung created
> the *Juche ideology*. Kim Il Sung wanted to create his own
> system of self-reliance. Finally, in December 1959,
> Kim Il Sung began to comment on the *Juche ideology*."
> —Sylwia Szyc, Polish researcher of North Korea

At the same time, in Romania, some North Korean war orphans living in Târgoviște had relationships with Romanian women. At that time, if they were found dating a foreigner in Romania, they had to be repatriated to North Korea immediately. This was why Georgeta Mircioiu had secretly dated Cho Chung Ho for four years before marrying him.

Other mixed couples were also dating in secret. The repatriation of the North Korean partner would mean having to separate. However, love between two people does not disappear just because the authorities interfere with the relationship.

After hearing that they would soon be repatriated, some North Korean war orphans escaped from the dormitory. They moved to other cities and kept a low profile. One of them later got married, started a family, and returned to Târgoviște to work as a taxi driver.

> "In Romania, a young man hopped over the fence of the
> Korea People's School dormitory. Teachers tried to catch
> the youth, but they were unsuccessful.
> I know that the reason the young man ran away was
> because of a young woman. It must have been difficult for
> a Romanian woman and a North Korean man to live
> together, because it was easy to spot them.
> Eventually, the two got married and had a child. I heard
> only that someone happened to see them in a taxi. No one

knew where they lived. Maybe they should have continued to live a wandering life, like gypsies."

— Jean-Pierre Thomas, janitor at the Korea People's School in Romania

I tried in several ways to find the couple, but I was unable to do so. The couple, who must have had to live under intense surveillance, somehow remained elusive. Although I couldn't find the North Korean man during my research in Romania, I had a feeling he was watching us from somewhere. I left Romania hoping that the man had a peaceful life. He had surrendered his ties to his country and homeland for freedom and love.

CLOSED GROUP SOCIETY

By 1959, all North Korean students, engineers, and war orphans had been ordered to return to North Korea. Between 1960 and 1962, almost all North Korean college students were repatriated. There were no more North Koreans left in Europe.

However, the very time of these repatriations was also the period when the most North Korean war orphans escaped from the dormitories. Some North Korean children seem to have been unsure whether to try to escape the repatriation or to stay with the group.

Aside from the war orphans, there were many North Korean students at the time who wanted to study advanced technology at Eastern European universities. The North Korean authorities' repatriation order applied equally to college students. Even so, a few North Korean college students refused to be repatriated and applied for asylum.

For North Korean war orphans and college students who grew up influenced by European culture, the sudden repatriation order was a violation of their freedom. Especially for the war orphans who lived with Europeans as in a family, the order to repatriate meant the tragedy of having to part with their families. Not a few people struggled between the sense of duty to be loyal to the party's orders and the sadness of having to part with the people they loved.

In Siret, Romania, the school was turned upside down because, on the day of repatriation, one North Korean war orphan did not board the train to return home. Instead, the child fled into the mountains.

Mircioiu was at the scene at the time. She said:

"I can't remember the child's name, but he was ill and was recuperating in the countryside. There, a janitor was very fond of the child. He had also lost his wife and family and was living alone. Over time, the man and the child became closer. The man treated the boy like he was his own son. Then, in 1959, the decision came to repatriate the children, and the news reached the man. Sad that the child he had cared for like his own had to return to North Korea, he told the child seriously: 'Don't go back to North Korea, I'll be your father. Why don't you stay in Romania and live with me?' The child answered, 'I want you to be my father.' Eventually, the two decided to live together in Romania."

The Romanian man immediately initiated a formal adoption process, hoping to raise the child as his son. However, the North Korean authorities did not allow this. The man and the child alike were heartbroken.

On the day he was to be repatriated, the eight-year-old child climbed over the dormitory wall, saying he would not return to North Korea.

It was the day when hundreds of children in the dormitory were scheduled to take the train back to North Korea. The child escaped over the fence just before the train left. The child ran away on foot toward the mountains for about 10 kilometers.

North Korean teachers and supervisors were desperate to find the child. His conduct was considered treason. Teachers ordered all the North Korean children waiting to board the train to pursue the escaped child.

Georgeta Mircioiu recalled:

"All the children were wearing sharp-looking uniforms as they were going back to North Korea, but they had to go find the kid who ran away.
It was cloudy that day, and then it rained. Hundreds of children ran in search of the escaped child, panting through the mud and rain. Eventually, they found the child hiding in the woods.
When they came back to school, their beautiful clothes were muddy, and their bodies were covered in sweat. Suddenly, the children grew angry and surrounded and beat the child. None of the teachers even stepped in to stop the collective beating of this child, who was kicked and punched in the face. The child was beaten so badly that his leg was broken.
In the end, the child was taken to North Korea without proper treatment. After the children returned to North Korea, they sent news that the child had become disabled. He was probably crippled for the rest of his life."

GROUP DEFECTION OF NORTH KOREAN COLLEGE STUDENTS IN BULGARIA

In the early 1960s, North Korean students started defecting. The best-known case was the group defection of North Korean college students in Bulgaria. In August 1962, instead of returning to North Korea, four North Korean students enrolled at Sofia University planned to seek asylum in Bulgaria. Their main motivation was their opposition to the Kim Il Sung dictatorship.

However, the asylum plan leaked out in advance, and the four students were abducted by North Korean agents. North Korean authorities ordered that the four be sent home immediately. But the four students escaped from the North Korean embassy where they were being detained. They fled to Mount Vitosha, near Sofia. They spent several days in the mountains battling the cold before being captured again by North Korean agents. They were detained at the North Korean embassy in Bulgaria.

This situation was known to the outside, and—in an unprecedented move—the Bulgarian government granted the North Korean students asylum. The four college students who were detained in the North Korean embassy were eventually released and placed under the protection of the Bulgarian government. Concerned that other North Korean students abroad would defect, Pyongyang froze diplomatic relations with Bulgaria for six years.

"There may have been a number of reasons why this happened, but one of them was that in the early 1960s, Kim Il Sung wanted to abandon the Soviet Union and develop closer ties with Mao Zedong in China.
"Relations with Soviet-dominated Eastern Europe were not good. The North Korean authorities protested strongly and even cut diplomatic ties with Bulgaria, because they feared that similar defections would occur.
But in reality, Kim Il Sung did not want students with European influences to come back to North Korea at the time. This was because they were cumbersome for Kim, who tried to rule North Korea in his own way."

— Jordan Baev, Bulgarian historian

The Bulgarian government granted citizenship to the four North Korean students. They were also guaranteed a high standard of education and living. One of the students, Lee Sang-jong, married a Bulgarian woman, had children, and lived in Bulgaria for the rest of his life. He died in 2014.

Another of the students, Han Sang-jik, who came to Bulgaria as an engineering student, fell in love with a Bulgarian woman, and got married. Because he was granted Bulgarian citizenship, he was able to avoid becoming a refugee. However, the students were never again allowed to visit their parents and siblings whom they had left behind in North Korea.

During the interview process, I met Han Sang-jik's son-in-law, Mitko Nikolov. Nikolov, who lives in Bankya, not far from Sofia, still has fond memories of his father-in-law.

Lee Sang-jong (far right, in the back row) and Han Sang-jik (far left, in the back row), two of the students seeking asylum in Bulgaria. The two settled in Bulgaria. Neither of them ever set foot on North Korean soil again.

"My father-in-law, Han Sang-jik, was a really nice person. He had been friends with Lee Sang-jong, who was exiled due to the escape of a North Korean student.
On Lunar New Year's Day and Chuseok (a Korean harvest festival), our families used to gather to hold ancestral rites and enjoy food together. At that time, they were the only North Koreans remaining in Bulgaria.
He had family in North Korea, and he always said that he wanted to see them. He said he wanted to visit his hometown at least once before he died, but in the end, he died without being able to set foot in his hometown."

— Mitko Nikolov, son-in-law of Han Sang-jik

The defection of North Korean students in Bulgaria was a story of courageous people who did not give up trying to escape to freedom, despite the humiliation of being abducted twice by North Korean agents. The case also showed the brutal nature of the North Korean regime, which tried to suppress and control even family love and personal feelings. Those who chose freedom had no homeland to return to.

1962: THE YEAR NORTH KOREA CLOSED ITS DOORS

What really happened in North Korea from the 1950s to the early 1960s? Understanding that period holds the key to understanding North Korea's present and future. During the 10 years in which North Korean war orphans were staying in Europe, major events took place in North Korea. It was a time of great change and challenge for North Korea and an age of possibility.

If North Korea had remained more closely aligned with the rest of the socialist bloc instead of following Kim Il Sung's increasingly dogmatic policies, the world would have been very different. In that respect, examining this period helps explain why Kim's monolithic ideology system was created and still governs North Korean society.

Even as it entrusted its children to foreign countries under difficult circumstances, North Korea thoroughly indoctrinated the children to worship Kim Il Sung. Before the *Juche ideology* was established, the North Korean children in Romania were being raised into a squadron of Kim Il Sung loyalists through ceremonial training. The Soviets wanted those children to be Stalin's, but they grew up to be Kim Il Sung's. However, Kim could not just leave alone the North Korean war orphans who had tasted European freedom. To him, freedom and individualism were never acceptable values. That was why the children were suddenly repatriated to North Korea and disappeared.

Kim Il Sung was someone who could abandon these children if the purpose was to strengthen his regime. That explains why the existence of the war orphans is still not properly acknowledged within North Korea and does not appear in official histories.

From the 1960s to the late 1980s, South and North Korea entered into a systemic competition. In the process, the existence of North Korean war orphans in Eastern Europe was detected by South Korean intelligence. Coincidentally, the reason South Korea tried to hide the presence of North Korean orphans in Eastern Europe was because it had an inferiority complex on that issue. Unlike North Korea, South Korea addressed its own war orphan crisis by facilitating overseas adoption.

> "South Korea sent children for adoption through Holt (an international adoption agency), and North Korea entrusted education to other socialist countries. South Korea made adoptive parents, while North Korea left (the kids) in their uncle's house for a while."
>
> — Haeseong Lee, professor of Korean language, University of Wrocław, Poland

South Korea's method of placing war orphans with families through overseas adoptions has resulted in numerous children being adopted. This is where South Korea's stigma of being an orphan exporter originated. According to known data, 500,000 children worldwide have been adopted abroad since World War II. Of these, about 200,000 were from South Korea. This means that 40 percent of the world's overseas adopted children are from the Republic of Korea.

The North Korean war orphans' education in Eastern Europe serves as a mirror for South Korea to reflect on the overseas adoption policy it chose. Meanwhile, from the North's perspective, the history of overseas migration of war orphans was nothing to be proud of.

Dreaming of a *Juche paradise* on earth, North Korea rejected all foreign ideologies and cultures. The isolated state system in North Korea that has survived to this day originated in the late 1950s. The reasons North Korea chose a path completely different from other communist countries in the world are all related to this period.

More objective data has recently been released. This concerns the 1958 group exile of North Korean students at the Russian State University of Cinematography (VGIK). In 2015, a South Korean daily newspaper, The Hankyoreh, published a black-and-white photo taken in November 1956 in front of the VGIK dormitory. The main figures in the photo were all North Korean state-funded college students—elite intellectuals who had promising futures in cinema. After they took this picture, they disappeared from the school. Indeed, out of the 10 North Korean students who were attending film schools in the Soviet Union in 1958, eight renounced their North Korean citizenship and applied for asylum.

When the students applied for asylum, the North Korean authorities branded them traitors. But the students never betrayed their country. It was only Kim Il Sung and his loyalists that they turned against.

Although they applied for asylum, they did not obtain Soviet citizenship. Six out of eight asylum-seekers chose the disastrous fate of being stateless. They had chosen the life of a rootless wanderer, who had neither a country to return to nor one to believe in. They never gave up their socialist ideals.

What they abandoned was not an ideal but a distorted system that worshiped the leader like an idol. They objected to the North Korean cult of personality surrounding Kim Il Sung, which expanded further in the late 1950s.

After Stalin's death in 1953, expressions of the cult of personality became much less tolerated in the Soviet Union. The Stalinist tyranny involved political purges and repression. In the end, it was only a matter of time before Khrushchev, who fiercely criticized Stalin's reign of terror, and Kim Il Sung, who tried to build his own kingdom in the northern half of Korea, clashed.

However, the Soviet authorities, not wanting to disrupt socialist solidarity, could not actively help the "young refugees." They even feared that the eight refugees might unite and engage in collective action. As a result, the eight young men were separated and dispersed across the vastness of Russia. And they lived unhappy lives.

The country they left in 1952 in order to learn and devote themselves to advanced civilization was frozen. Within the only party, the Workers' Party of Korea, the internal democracy that kept checks and balances between factions disappeared. On December 15, 1955, Pak Heon-yeong of the Southern branch of the Workers' Party of Korea was executed, and in June and August 1956, the Yan'an faction and Soviet faction were purged.

Ri Sang-jo, the North Korean ambassador to Russia, who had been close with (North Korean) overseas students in a free atmosphere, was forced out of office in 1957 after being accused of being part of the Yan'an faction.

When the harsh winter came in North Korea, spring was blooming in the Soviet Union, the home of the Communist Party. Stalin... died in 1953. News of Nikita Khrushchev's criticism of Stalin's cult of personality at the 20th Congress of the Communist Party of the Soviet Union in February 1956 circulated among North Korean college students abroad and elites.

Heo Woong-bae, who was in the same department, did not return after leaving the university. On November 27, 1957, he attended the Korea International Student Convention in Moscow, criticized Kim Il Sung's cult of personality, and then fled.

Han Dae-yong was in the same position as Heo Woong-bae, but he couldn't say anything. Heo Woong-bae, who was dragged off the podium by rivals, fled. After the embassy pursued him and persuaded him to come back, he returned to the embassy on his own but was soon detained. Then he escaped through the embassy bathroom window, ran into a subway station and appealed to the station staff for help. He was handed over to the Soviet authorities but fled with his lover, Choi Seon-ok, another student at a medical school.

— The Hankyoreh (a South Korean daily newspaper), September 5, 2015

At that time, North Korea was in the midst of the anti-factionalist campaign. Those who opposed or showed even the slightest negative perception of Kim Il Sung's cult of personality had to be purged, along with their families. The idea was that "if you see weeds sprouting, you have to dig up the roots."

Sylwia Szyc, a researcher affiliated with the Polish State Archives, argues that it was in this period of defections and purges that North Korea chose the path of a "hermit kingdom" that cut ties with the international community. It also coincides with the period when Kim Il Sung's *Juche ideology* began as a means of social control, as well as the establishment of a surveillance system over the population and the campaign in North Korea to exclude foreigners.

In fact, such a monitoring system also operated in Eastern Europe among the North Korean children. They monitored each other's words and actions, and they immediately reported suspicious actions to teachers and administrators. There was no way to know which of the North Korean teachers were also secret informants.

The Cold War era began when the world was already divided into blocs of capitalism and communism. It was also a period in which a new variable, China, emerged in the international political order. The transition from a bipolar system to a multipolar system that included China was a golden opportunity for Kim Il Sung to expand his power. Kim cleverly balanced himself between the Soviet Union and China. And the results were mostly as Kim intended.

The 1958 defection of eight North Korean elite students attending film school in Moscow demonstrated just how opposed to Kim Il Sung many North Korean intellectuals were.

"Since 1959, North Korea has implemented a policy of blocking all forms of culture and politics from outside. The movement of foreign diplomats in North Korea began to be restricted, and their phone calls were monitored. Foreign diplomats could not even have direct contact with Pyongyang citizens. If a North Korean citizen happened to meet a European diplomat on the street, he had to immediately stop talking and report the matter to the relevant authorities. That marked the beginning of the era of North Korea's isolation."

— Sylwia Szyc, Polish researcher of North Korea

CHAPTER 5

FROM STALIN'S CHILDREN TO KIM IL SUNG'S CHILDREN

KISS MY YOUNGER BROTHER ANDRZEJ...

As 1956 passed, the children sensed that it was time for them to return. Like migratory birds that know when the seasons change and when to leave, the children once again prepared for a long trip. However, the separation was not easy for them; they had come to Europe at a young age to meet new guardians, friends, and teachers who guided them through life.

It was just as difficult for teachers and friends in Eastern Europe, who had to say goodbye to the North Korean children. Stanisław Wachal, a physical education teacher who lived with 1,400 North Korean children in Prochowice, Poland, recalled the moment of farewell.

> Did you know that the North Korean children were going back to North Korea when you left Prochowice?
> "I think I knew. Suddenly the children started giving out pictures of themselves. It was kind of a hint that it was time to part."
> How did you feel then?
> "It was so sad that I felt sick."
> Were you that close with them?
> "Of course! We were like a family."

In Czechoslovakia, too, the children found it hard to say goodbye to Marie Kopecká, who had become like a sister to them. None of the children knew why they had to go, or where they were headed. In some cases, younger children created disturbances and said they would not return to North Korea.

Jeong Yeong-hee loved and cherished Andrzej, a baby boy who lived in Prochowice, Poland, as if he were her younger brother. Even after returning to North Korea, she sent a letter saying, "I miss my brother Andrzej. Is Andrzej doing well? I want to see him. From far away, now, as I finish this letter, I send Andrzej a big kiss."

"You don't know how many times I cried when I heard that a child was trying to catch a cold by rolling in the snow. He thought that he would not have to take the 'North Song' (repatriation) train if he got sick. Did he really want not to go that much? But there was no way the children could stay."

— Marie Kopecká, teacher of North Korean war orphans in Valeč

More North Korean war orphans lived in Prochowice, Poland, than in any other location in Eastern Europe. It was like a desert island, as the landscape cut them off from the outside. They created their own community there without any outside influence. The story

In Hungary, the North Korean war orphans took classes with Hungarian students at a regular school to help them quickly adapt to life in Europe. 1955.

of a Polish child named Andrzej and Jeong Yeong-hee, a North Korean girl who lived in this village, shows how harmoniously people who were of different colors and who spoke different languages were able to live together.

Yeong-hee, who was in her early teens, was living in the North Korean children's dormitory in Prochowice. At that time, a Polish woman named Florentina was in charge of the dormitory kitchen.

One day, Yeong-hee asked Florentina if she could help out in the kitchen. For Florentina, Yeong-hee cut potatoes, peeled onions, and washed the dishes. Over time, Yeong-hee and Florentina became as close as sisters.

A few years later, Florentina got married and, a year after that, had a boy. The boy's name was Andrzej. As Florentina was often busy working in the kitchen, Yeong-hee began to take care of Andrzej.

Later, she made a Korean-style baby sling and carried Andrzej on her back. Because Europeans don't carry babies on their backs, she looked odd doing that in Poland. However, Florentina continued to entrust the baby to Yeong-hee. She knew that Yeong-hee would take care of Andrzej as if he were her own younger brother.

During our research in Prochowice, we located a picture of a North Korean girl holding a Polish baby boy in her arms. They looked friendly, like brothers and sisters. We later learned that the people in the photo were none other than Jeong Yeong-hee and Andrzej.

Later, after returning to North Korea, Yeong-hee asked about Andrzej every time she wrote Florentina a letter.

Yeong-hee missed Andrzej. To Yeong-hee, who had no parents or siblings left, Andrzej was like family. The girl's expression in the photo was peaceful and happy, evoking a time when people met without any material or other calculated motives.

On the train heading back to North Korea, Yeong-hee wrote to the Polish family:

> "To my respectful and loving Mom and Dad,
> I was so sad to be separated from my beloved mother, father, and younger brother. I kept thinking about you after I left. My heart aches at the thought of separating like this and that we will never be able to meet again. I will never forget my second country, Poland, and my younger brother, Andrzej, whom I always took care of. I am writing this letter while looking at the beautiful scenery outside the window.

Sorry for the messy writing. The train is shaking. This concludes my short letter. Goodbye.

Best regards to all family members.

From Baby Monkey (Jeong Yeong-hee's nickname) on the train"

— Quoted from "The Płakowice Orphanage for the War-Orphans from North Korea in Poland, Remained in Józef Borowiec's Memories," an essay (in Korean) by Haeseong Lee, professor of Korean language, University of Wrocław, Poland

However, by 1962, Yeong-hee's letters were being intercepted by the North Korean authorities and could no longer reach Poland. Florentina from Prochowice, who hoped to one day hear again from Yeong-hee, waited 60 years without getting another letter. Yeong-hee had long wanted to see Andrzej again but could not. Their touching story has been buried in time.

Andrzej must now be in his late 60s. We were not able to locate him; all we heard was that he became a railroad station worker and has since retired.

THE MOMENT OF PARTING COMES

Just before their departure, the children from North Korea arranged their farewells in their own way. They chatted all night with their European friends and took commemorative photos with the teachers who took care of them like their own children. At that time, it was expensive to take even a single photo. The children either worked part-time jobs or raised money together to take pictures.

In the course of our research journey from Poland to our final destination, Bulgaria, we discovered about 100 photos that the war orphans had enclosed with their letters to Europe after returning to North Korea.

In their letters, the children asked their European friends not to forget them. On the back of the photo are messages recalling the children's happy memories in Europe. These short messages resonated deeply. They wrote their names along with the words "Thank you," "I will never forget," and "I miss you."

"We will never forget Mother Vasa."

All the children had many memories of the places they lived in Eastern Europe. They spent between five and 10 of their formative years there. However, even in the relatively free atmosphere of Europe, the children were not free. They all had to wake up at the

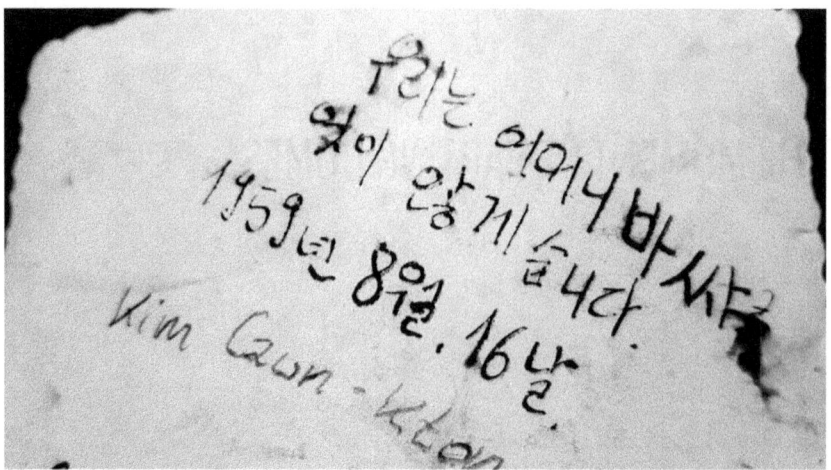

A message on the back of a photo sent by a North Korean war orphan who had lived in Poland and then returned to North Korea.

same time, eat together in the cafeteria, and go to bed at the same time.

Such practices were unfamiliar to Europeans. Collective-style education was applied in European communist countries, but not to such an extreme degree. For example, for Europeans it was unimaginable to put 10-year-old children through ceremonial training and military parades. This was not part of a proper education for young children.

However, as such closed and collective education intensified, teachers and friends in Europe secretly bonded with the children. In some cases, they befriended children who had lost their parents, and they became like foster family members. No state or party could control such emotions. Rather, more and more people felt sympathy for the North Korean children who had to live in such pitiful conditions.

> "The children seem to have lived with sadness in their hearts. But they hid their sadness from others. Perhaps they learned that from the North Korean teachers. Children had to cry in places where no one else could see them. So I think they felt more pitiful.
> In Bulgaria, teachers instructed the Bulgarian students not to say anything that could hurt them (the North Korean war orphans). In particular, the word 'orphan' was a word that was never to be used inside or outside school."
> — Dianka Ivanova, Bulgarian teacher

Sometimes the European teachers took their students to the mountains or rivers to teach them outdoors. In this way, they tried to ease the children's minds. At that time, there was no swimming pool, so children mainly went to the river to swim or play.

Then there was an accident. That day, a 10-year-old girl named Ri Nam-ju, living in Parvomay, Bulgaria, was playing in the river with the other children. Suddenly, screams were heard. It was Ri Nam-ju's voice. Two sisters, Ri Hyeon-ju and Ri Yeon-ju, found her struggling and drowning. The two sisters threw their shoes and clothes into the water to try to save the child. But it was too late. The incident shocked the Bulgarian and the North Korean teachers alike, as well as the residents of the village. Everyone was sad to hear that the little girl had drowned.

The mayor of Parvomay awarded medals to the two sisters who made an all-out effort to save the drowning girl. The sisters became town celebrities as a result. They were also awarded a prize of 100 levs. This was a lot of money at the time. However, even though the sisters were at an age when they might have wanted to wear nice clothes and eat delicious food, they decided instead to use the prize money to take photos with the villagers. This was because they wanted to maintain their friendships with the locals. That was how the North Korean children felt right before they were repatriated to

North Korea.

This was why their Bulgarian friends were able to preserve their detailed memories of the North Korean children, even 60 years later. They had shared so many experiences and created so many memories. And through the photos they left behind, memories remained fresh. This is why the elderly Bulgarians were able to remember the names of their North Korean friends from long ago, as well as details about their appearance and personality.

REPATRIATION TRAIN

The Eastern Europeans thought their North Korean friends would always be around; they did not know why the war orphans had to return. The North Korean children were repatriated with almost no advance notice. Maria Yamalieva, who studied alongside the North Korean children in Parvomay, Bulgaria, recalled the times just before the children were repatriated. The friend she missed the most was a girl named Kim Jin-woo. She said that she and Jin-woo cried for several days, as each regretted having to part.

> Do you remember saying farewell to a friend named Kim Jin-woo?
> "How could I forget? Long black hair, red cheeks… She was always smiling. She was my best friend. We sat side by side at the same desk and studied. We were mates. We ate together and she got along well with my mother and grandmother. She was like family. I cried a lot when I parted from her. One day a train came and took all the children and left. Since then, there has been no contact.
> A lot of time has passed, but I still can't forget that friend."

Lilka Anatasova also remembered the day of repatriation in great detail. It was the last time she was with her friend, a girl named Park In-suk. She had never imagined that the farewell to her friend that day would be forever.

> "I remember saying goodbye to a friend named Park In-suk. She must be old now. She was the same age as me, so she must be about 77 years old now."

Do you still remember her face?

> "Of course I remember. I remember the last time I saw her. There was also a photo of us looking at the lake together in front of the post office. We even talked for an hour before the train left on the last day."

What did you talk about?

> "It's been so many years that I can't remember the exact conversation. We reminded each other of the days we spent together and promised to see each other again. I said it would be really nice to see her again.
> But unfortunately, we never met again."

The repatriation of North Korean children from Bulgaria in 1959 proceeded like a military operation. The sudden parting was shocking and sad for the war orphans' European friends, who had lived with them in those years.

The Trans-Siberian train carrying the children began its long journey toward Pyongyang. That was the children's last appearance.

> "I want people to remember this history as it was. It was human beings meeting each other. Between them, love, friendship, and human connections arose. Their stories have more power than politics or propaganda. Their life was like life on a desert island.

Like people living on desert islands, they were separated from the outside world. Because they were together, they were not lonely and could be happy."

— Jolanta Krysowata, Polish documentary director

For the children who had already lived in Eastern Europe, some for nearly 10 years, their respective home bases there were like their second hometown. Many years have passed since the children left, but there are still people in Europe who miss them. It was heartbreaking to think that the children who returned to North Korea would have lived their lives without knowing this. The children never came back, but did they still miss Europe? Perhaps this second hometown remained forever in the hearts of those children. I wonder if, in their place, I would have lived the rest of my life with a second hometown in my heart.

KIM IL SUNG FEARED THE CHILDREN'S RETURN

Many clues in the repatriation process help us understand the context surrounding the orphans who lived in Europe. The anti-Soviet resistance in Eastern Europe in the mid-1950s put Kim Il Sung in a difficult position. Kim had to address the risks posed by nearly 10,000 children with relatively free European values. He thought that if the children were left in Europe, many of them would rebel against his regime. However, simply repatriating them to North Korea risked planting the seeds of an anti-regime movement.

It was necessary to somehow crack down on the nearly 10,000 educated youth who were influenced by the liberalization movement taking place in Europe. This time, Kim Il Sung's regime made a dual diplomatic gesture. While touting their humanitarianism to the outside world, in reality they were monitoring and controlling the children.

The orphans wrote letters to Polish teacher Stanisław Wachal after returning to North Korea. These letters gave clues as to how the children reintegrated into North Korean society after their return.

"As soon as the train crossed the North Korean-Chinese border, it stopped at a small station and started dropping off the children. The children could not stay together as they had in Poland.

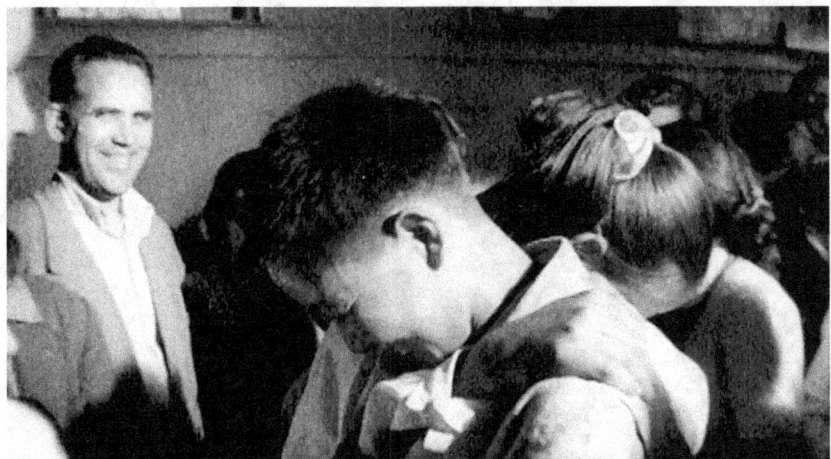

In 1959, a repatriation train in Bulgaria with North Korean war orphans headed off for Pyongyang. Children gave one last hug goodbye before boarding the train.

The children's letters said they were scattered all over North Korea. They dropped off each child separately at different stations. To keep the children apart, two of them were dropped off at this station and a few more at other stations.
The children had always lived together in Europe. I think Kim Il Sung planned to disperse the children like that from the moment they entered North Korea."
— Stanisław Wachal, Polish teacher

In Eastern Europe, the war orphans had long lived together in dormitories, but when they returned to North Korea, they had no chance to remain together. In many cases, they never saw each other again.

The children were put under strict segregation and surveillance. They were stigmatized as leading a counter-revolutionary existence imbued with foreign cultures and ideas.

Eventually, the children were put to work in coal mines and other types of mines, where they lived miserable lives.

The children had no opportunity to apply the advanced European technology and culture they had learned. They returned to the place where they were born and raised, but it was no longer the home they dreamed of. They had to spend their whole lives longing for the "second hometown" they had in their hearts.

FROM STALIN'S CHILDREN TO KIM IL SUNG'S CHILDREN 229

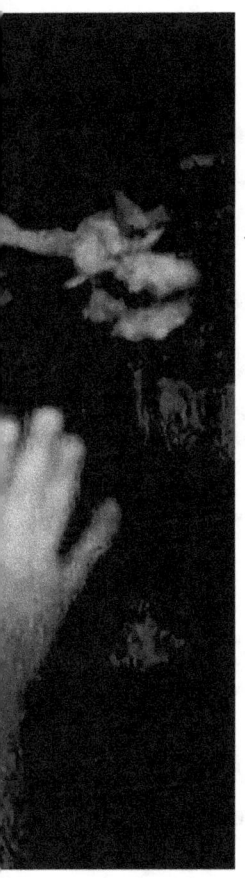

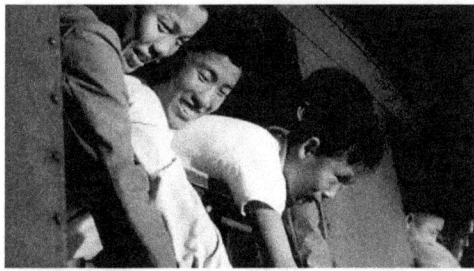

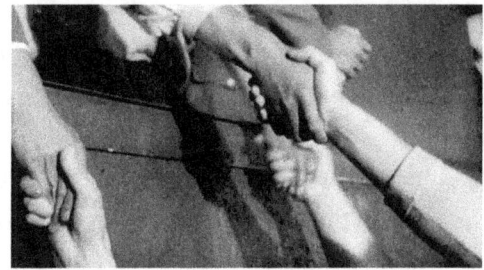

A repatriation train carrying North Korean children. The North Korean war orphans said goodbye to the Bulgarian students who were sent off to the station. (1959, Sofia)

MEETING A NORTH KOREAN WAR ORPHAN IN PYONGYANG

After the North Korean children left, the sense of loss felt by their Eastern European friends and teachers was unimaginable. The Eastern Europeans tried to keep in touch with their North Korean friends through letters, and after that correspondence was cut off, they tried to hold on to their memories.

> "It's really not easy for me to forgive North Korea's education policy. They teach their children to live first for their country and second for their party. Third and last comes family.
> Based on such values, Cho Chung Ho was sent to a coal mine and had to live for the country and the party, not his family. Despite having lung disease, my husband spent his days in a coal mine. In the end, he had to sacrifice himself for the party."
> — Georgeta Mircioiu

The Polish embassy in Pyongyang secretly attempted to track down the North Korean children who had previously lived in Poland. This initiative seems to have been in response to the many inquiries Polish citizens made concerning the children's whereabouts. To the Poles who knew them well, the North Korean orphans were like family. The Poles could not comprehend why the children whom they had cared for so affectionately had returned to North Korea and could no longer even be contacted. Recently, in Poland, diplomatic documents were released detailing the life in Pyongyang of a Polish ambassador to North Korea who took his post around 1963.

One incident the ambassador recorded was of particular interest. One day, he was walking down the streets of Pyongyang. Suddenly, a young man ran up to the ambassador. "Are you from Poland?" he asked. The ambassador was caught off guard. Just as surprising as the question was the fact that the young North Korean was speaking Polish. In fact, his accent was almost perfect.

The ambassador asked the young man: "How do you speak Polish so well? This is the first time I've come across anyone in North Korea who speaks Polish as well as you." The young North Korean man answered in Polish: "I used to live in Poland when I was young. There I learned from Polish teachers."

The Polish ambassador knew that in the 1960s, there was only one way a North Korean child could have lived in Poland—if he had been housed there as a North Korean war orphan. The Polish ambassador could not believe that one of the North Korean war orphans he had been looking for was standing in front of him. The ambassador grasped the young North Korean's arm, hoping to have a longer conversation. However, the young man shook off the ambassador and ran off. The ambassador ran after the young man but could not catch up to him.

As he watched the man disappear, the Polish ambassador had complicated thoughts: "Why did he approach me?" "Maybe the young man wanted to speak Polish?" and "Is it possible that he missed Poland that much?"

From that day on, the Polish ambassador could not forget the young man. Although it was a brief meeting, the young man must have been speaking Polish for the first time in a long while. Thinking of the friends he studied with and the teachers who were like his foster parents, the young man might have had happy memories. And perhaps the young man hoped to learn how his teachers and friends living in Poland were doing. Like the Polish-speaking young North Korean man, there are people living somewhere in North Korea who can speak Bulgarian, Romanian, Czech, or Hungarian, and they have a second hometown to return to.

With that in mind, the ambassador wrote accounts of his experiences, noting that he hoped it would be helpful if someone found them in the future.

Where was the paradise on earth that Kim Il Sung spoke of, where the people enjoyed equality and lived a happy life? In North Korea in the 1960s, the reality was that even love or friendship would be punished without mercy if it was perceived as a danger to the Kim Il Sung regime. Just talking to a foreigner on the street would cause a North Korean to be placed under official surveillance. All foreign phone calls were tapped, and people were either purged or sent to political prison camps for a careless word.

This ideology of excluding foreigners went hand in hand with Kim's one-party dictatorship and cult of personality. The closed and warped systems of the North Korean state all began to take shape from this period.

North Korea's ideology of excluding foreigners led to an obsession with racial purity. Surprisingly, this notion still dominates North Korean society to this day. Humanity has already learned from the Nazis how cruel the consequences of this obsession could be.

A LAST MESSAGE TO A FRIEND IN NORTH KOREA

Seventy years have passed since the North Korean war orphans lived in Europe. Most of those who retained the memories of that time are now dead. Fortunately, in the course of this research, we found 12 living friends of the war orphans. They are three teachers who taught North Korean children in Valeč, Czechoslovakia (now the Czech Republic), and in Prochowice and Otwock, Poland; six classmates and one teacher who played with North Korean children at the same school in Bulgaria; and one teacher from Romania. Georgeta Mircioiu was the biggest asset we unearthed in the course of this research. Through her, I was able to get as close as possible to the North Korean children who lived in Eastern Europe in the 1950s.

Time stops for no one. These Eastern Europeans we met are now all elderly people in their 80s or older, and most of them are now of limited mobility. Still, it was fortunate to have found them and documented their vivid recollections in a documentary. Just a little bit later, and it might already have been too late to record their memories.

I headed to Parvomay, Bulgaria, for the last shoot. Seven elderly Bulgarians who knew the North Korean orphans were waiting there to be interviewed. Though they were nearly 80 years old and could not even stand for long, they all made themselves available. They poured out all their memories. They were well aware that their testimony would be their last. Looking back now, it was a great honor for me to experience that moment.

The filming of our documentary ended with an interview with those in Bulgaria who had studied and played with the North Korean children. My long journey to find the traces of North Korean war orphans in Eastern Europe in the 1950s had come to an end. I asked them to record a message for their friends who might be living in North Korea.

One by one, they sat in front of the camera and left a final message, as if their friends were in front of them. They gave it their best, in the hope that their friends in North Korea might be able to receive their message through this film.

If this film can enter North Korea, perhaps those North Koreans will be able to see the messages conveyed by their old Eastern European friends. Somewhere in North Korea, there might be someone who remembers their faces and their voices. With this glimmer of hope in mind, I captured their messages on camera.

> "When we parted, I asked them to come back to Bulgaria to meet me again, but I got no response. We talked about a happy future together, but I heard no news about what happened to them."
>
> "My friend, if you are alive, please contact me. I hope you find a way to contact me. I am also very curious about how you are doing. I wish you a healthy life, happiness, and success always."
>
> "The first Korean friend I met was Choi Byung-ho. He was a skinny kid. I was really good friends with him. He also taught me how to speak and write in Korean. I send my regards to Choi Byung-ho. Byung-ho, if you are still alive, I hope you receive my regards. Do you remember when you came to my house? I remember you having fun looking around our house. You were amazed at how we

lived. We are all similar people. The years go by so fast. When did we get so old?"

"My dear friend, it is very sad that I had no way of contacting you after we parted. But I will never forget the memories I had with you and the splendid childhood we had together."

"Nak-won, I hope you are in good health. I want to meet you before I die. I want to tell both Park In-suk and Jeon Nak-won that I have not forgotten them. I will never forget them as long as I live. I hope they are healthy. I wish them a happy life and also that they have many children. Children who are just like they were when they were young. The kids from Korea back then were really nice."

"I send my sincere greetings to Won Cheong-dong. I wish him success and good health. I hope to see you again."

— Stanisław Wachal, Polish teacher

"I send the most beautiful greetings from Poland to Kim Young-hak. Do you still remember your elementary school days in Otwock? You were my best student. As your teacher, I always wish you the best of luck."

— Halina Dovek, Polish teacher

"To all of you in North Korea: if you happen to see this movie, and if you are alive and well, I hope you all live a healthy life and live to be over 100 years old. We will live in a healthy way too, so we can meet again. So goodbye, everyone, until we meet again!"

— From the movie *Kim Il Sung's Children*

LETTERS FROM NORTH KOREA

Even after they returned to North Korea, the children regarded their European residences as their real homes. The children addressed their letters "To Mom and Dad at home." They thought of each other like family. Writing letters, and hoping that they would meet again, were the only things that sustained them.

The sudden break in correspondence was a great shock and pain, both for the children who went back to North Korea and for their teachers and friends in Europe. The reason for releasing the letters they left is because of the addresses of the children written on the envelopes. If, in the future, the opportunity arises to trace the children's fates, I believe that the addresses on the envelopes will be a valuable resource.

> "In the first year the children returned to North Korea, they were free to send and receive letters. At that time, letters from the children from North Korea were piled up in bundles.
> However, after a year or two, I heard that the North had ordered a ban on the exchange of correspondence. This was because the children wrote unflattering information about North Korean society in their letters."
>
> — Stanisław Wachal, Polish teacher

FROM STALIN'S CHILDREN TO KIM IL SUNG'S CHILDREN 237

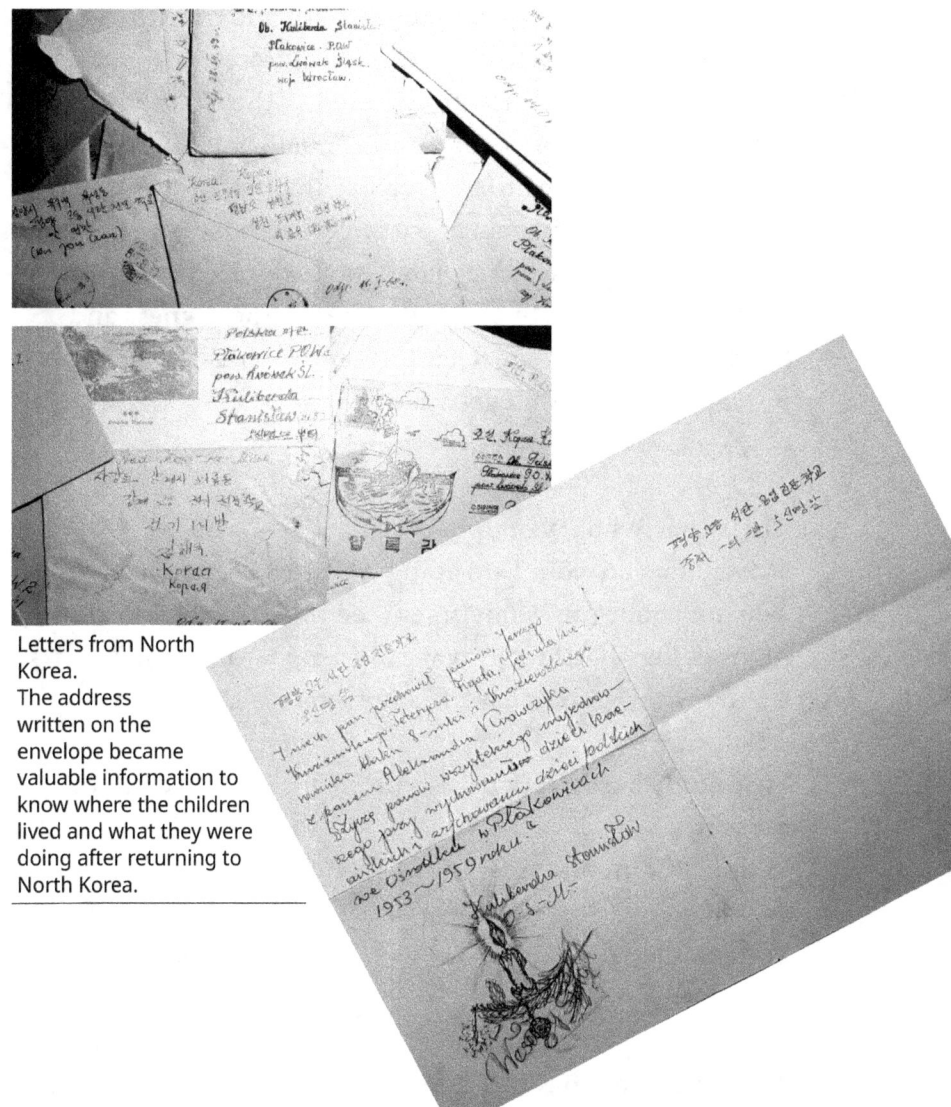

Letters from North Korea.
The address written on the envelope became valuable information to know where the children lived and what they were doing after returning to North Korea.

"The children went back to North Korea and tried to somehow get in touch with their Polish (foster) parents. That was a common intention shared by the children after they returned to North Korea from Poland in 1959, even though they lived in different environments.
They all suffered the pain of parting with those whom they had been close to in Poland. Some children overcame the trauma quickly, but most endured homesickness and longing for years. Some fell into a sense of frustration and loss, and they couldn't get out of it."

— Sylwia Szyc, Polish researcher of North Korea

"To Father, who I want to see
Father, how are you? I am doing well, too. Last night I had a dream about you. Sometimes I see you in my dreams. At times like that, I really want to go home, and I can't stand it. Maybe someday I'll come see you? Until then, stay healthy.
I will study hard, work hard, and live hard until I come to see you.
I think I will never forget the moment I lived with you.
So, I'm going to cut this short today.
To my father at home...."

— A letter from North Korea

After returning to North Korea between 1959 and 1962, many North Korean children who had lived in Poland always remembered to write one thing at the end of their letter:

"Father, Mother, please bring us to Poland."

Between 1951 and 1959, between 5,000 and 10,000 North Korean war orphans shared friendship and affection with local teachers and students while studying and living in Eastern Europe. Before being repatriated to North Korea, they learned the local language, got to know each other, and lived like family, or in some cases, as lovers. So for the children from North Korea, their Eastern European base was the "second hometown" in their hearts. The picture was taken from the sky of a beautiful rural landscape that I accidentally discovered while traveling to the village of Prochowice, Poland, where 1,400 North Korean war orphans had lived. It was called "New Forest."

THERE IS NO HOMETOWN IN THE WORLD THAT ONE CANNOT RETURN TO

We live in a globalized era, where everyone is connected. The borders that separate people are also becoming increasingly blurred. We can travel to the far corners of the globe, meet new people there, and share friendship and love. Even an unfamiliar place can, over time, become your home. So you can have two hometowns or even more.

When we meet people who are struggling, we help each other. If we have a lot, we enjoy sharing a little with others. That's how we live. But what if there is no home in this world to which one can return? It is very unfortunate that we cannot return to the happy memories we shared with our parents and siblings in our hometown. You should be able to return to your hometown.

Our long journey to trace the lives of North Korean war orphans in Eastern Europe in order to produce Kim Il Sung's Children is coming to an end. Every beginning also has an end, and every new encounter eventually involves a parting. However, from the point of view of nature and life, death is not the end but preparation for a new beginning.

After the nearly 10,000 war orphans returned to North Korea, the regime there has never disclosed any records about them or revealed the fate of even one of them. So my one wish is that this book will serve as a guide in finding out the orphans' hidden history.

I hope that one day, all their hidden stories will be fairly assessed and fully revealed. That was my purpose in writing this book. I dedicate this work to all the war orphans in the world and to all those who devoted their lives to them.

AWARDS AND RECOGNITIONS

2020　Rome International Movie Awards (Italy) The Best Documentary Winner

2020　Eastern Europe International Movie Awards Silver Award

2020　Cyrus International Film Festival of Toronto (Canada) Semi Finalist

2020　'Global Migration Film Festival' by UN International Organization of Migration Official Selection

2020　International New York Film Festival (US) Official Selection

2020　Nice International Film Festival (France) Official Selection

2020　Deptford Cinema On Demand (UK) Official Selection

2020　Golden Tree International Documentary Film Festival (Germany) Official Selection

2020　Tokyo-Lift Off Film Festival (Japan) Official Selection

2020　Santa Cruz International Film Festival (Argentina) Official Selection

2020　Polish International Film Festival (Poland) Official Selection

2020　Rasnov Film and Histories Festival (Romania) Official Selection

2020　Pyeongchang International Film Festival (South Korea) Official Selection

2020　Eastern Europe International Movie Awards Official Selection

2020　First-Time Filmmaker Film Festival (US) Official Selection

2020　National Archives of Korea (South Korea) Permanent Records Selection

ABOUT THE AUTHOR

Author Kim Deog-Young directed the documentary film *Kim Il Sung's Children* which traced the lives of North Korean orphans in Eastern Europe following the Korean War in the 1950s. The 15-year endeavor that started in 2004 includes interviews with 12 individuals who were friends and instructors of the North Korean orphans.

The testimonials and records featured in the film were disclosed to the world for the first time. The stories of pure love and friendship - unhampered by politics and ideology - resonated with numerous viewers. The film was assessed to have shed a new light on North Korean human rights issues by examining the development of North Korea's closed society.

The documentary film Kim Il Sung's Children was released in South Korea on June 25, 2020, the 70th anniversary of the start of the Korean War. It made official selections in 15 international film festivals, including the New York Film Festival and Nice International Film Festival; and it won Best Documentary Feature at the Rome International Movie Awards and Silver Award at Eastern Europe International Movie Awards. This book compiles numerous episodes from the production and additional records not included in the documentary film.

Kim made his debut as a film director in 1995 with Waning 1989. Kim's another film Farewell to the Factory (1999) made an official selection at Busan International Film Festival and was aired on Japan's NHK in 1999. Kim Il Sung's Children, released in 2020, was internationally acclaimed, making Kim South Korea's leading documentary film director.

Kim is the author of numerous written works, including Life Post Retirement, Haruki's Peter Cat and My Tonguidong Story. It's All Documentary, I'll Meet You There, Eurail Route, and Launching Life Part II. Kim's publication Walking the Greek Time was selected as a recommended reading by the Ministry of Culture and Tourism in 2012.

Employing books and films as creative outlets, Kim uncovers hidden stories of the world. Kim made a resolution to compile one book a year since his first publication in 2009, he has kept up with his promise to this day. He has a bachelor's and master's degree in philosophy from Sogang University.

documentary story
Email: docustory@gmail.com
Website: www.2twohomes.com
Facebook: www.facebook.com/altna84
Blog: blog.naver.com/altna84
Instagram: instagram.com/documentor1
Twitter: twitter.com/docuNbook

www.ingramcontent.com/pod-product-compliance
Lightning Source LLC
Chambersburg PA
CBHW070052080526
44586CB00013B/1025